Heroes, Villains & Victims

·OF BRADFORD·

Heroes, Villains & Victims

·OF BRADFORD·

Stephen Wade

breedon **books**
PUBLISHING

First published in Great Britain in 2008 by
The Breedon Books Publishing Company Limited
Breedon House, 3 The Parker Centre,
Derby, DE21 4SZ.

ISBN 978-1-85983-628-6

Printed and bound by Cromwell Press Ltd., Trowbridge, Wiltshire.

Contents

Acknowledgements

Thanks to John Styles for his work on Samuel Lister
and to Laura Carter for the drawings.

Preface

Bradford is currently famous for being the home of the National Museum of Photography, David Hockney and the Brontës. It also has the reputation in some quarters of being very much an Asian community, with a massive concentration of Asian Yorkshire folk. Historically it has been in competition with Leeds, its near neighbour, in terms of economics and the heritage industry. But, arguably, the great 'Worstedopolis' of Victorian England leads the way in the heritage industry and in its sense of the past.

It may seem hard to find the history beneath the large-scale building and the modern urban problems, but it is there, and not simply in Saltaire and Haworth. The Victorian city is still evident and is best seen on foot: the schools, parks, industrialists' houses, battle sites, churches and chapels still tell the exciting narrative of the Industrial Revolution.

But there is more to the city than the impressive architecture; this book is about the Bradford people who have made their mark in their chosen professions and careers. Some are household names like J.B. Priestley, while others are more obscure. One thing is remarkable, though: Bradford has always been a place of writers and artists, scholars and literary types. Many of these may not be well known today, but in their time they were widely read and always to be found in the newspapers. Such people were W. Riley, author of the phenomenal best-seller *Windyridge*, and Joseph Wright, the father of modern dialect studies.

As with all the cities and towns of the West Riding, there is a profound pride and a sense of place in Bradford that is very strong. Priestley, in his 1930s travel book *English Journey*, summed up one aspect of this: 'However poor you are in Bradford, you need never be walled in, bricked up, as a million folk must be in London. Those great bare heights, with a purity of sky above and behind them, are always there, waiting for you...There is no better country in England.'

There is also a presiding spirit behind this book: that of William Scruton, Victorian historian of Bradford, and a man to whom every writer on this fascinating place owes a debt of gratitude. He knew every scrap of local history, myth and folklore around the area, and one writer described him in this way: 'Mr Scruton has a proper reverence for old places, old families, and old associations, and in his remarks contrives to arouse a deep interest in the mind of the reader.' I devote a chapter to Mr Scruton in the following pages, and I hope that I also 'arouse a deep interest' in the stories of some of the people who have made Bradford the city it is today. I also include something on that other great historian from Bradford, Asa Briggs, famous for his books *Victorian Cities* and *Victorian Things*.

Of course, this book also has some villains among the heroes, and hopefully the stories of crime will tell the reader as much about the history of the city as the usual biographies of worthies such as W.E. Forster and Titus Salt. Here you can decide for yourself whether or not Jack the Ripper paid a murderous visit to Bradford, and how a young man escaped the noose back in the days of capital punishment.

In recent decades, Bradford has made the national headlines for the wrong reasons: shootings in the street, the nefarious murders by the Yorkshire Ripper and riots instilling fear into good citizens. We do not only have to look backwards to find gentler and more ordered times, because the fact is that the city has always had the crime in the streets and the political confrontations. But all those things have been a sign of vibrancy, social melioration and a healthy feeling for debate and discussion. There has been a fight for identity, and many of the people whose lives are told here played a major part in that struggle for certainty and cohesion.

Several writers' works have been extremely valuable in the preparation of this volume, notably the writings of Derek Lister, Bob Duckett, Marie Campbell and Gary Firth. John Styles's work on Lister the magistrate detective was invaluable. For the Brontës, I am indebted to many writers and scholars, and without the line drawings created by artists like Laura Carter I would not have had the variety I wanted in the illustrations.

ONE

Slaughter in Calverley

'Murder most foul, as in the best it is,
But this most foul, strange, and unnatural.'

Hamlet

In 1608 the play *A Yorkshire Tragedy* was published, and was printed as being written by William Shakespeare. Scholarship since then has shown that it was almost certainly not written by him. The story is in the popular Elizabethan genre of the domestic tragedy, and it is based on events at Calverley Hall, near Bradford, in 1605. These 'events' consisted of a man brutally murdering his own sons and stabbing his wife. It was a story with the same kind of melodramatic appeal as the Victorian sensation trial – full of violent rage and senseless blood-spilling, the work of a madman. It matched well with the current popularity of nasty and deranged Machiavellian revenge drama. But there was nothing melodramatic about the real events, and the killer in question has to rank as one of the very worst Bradford villains.

That was the one important difference between the literary tale and the story itself: the events really

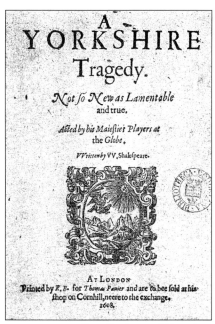

Frontispiece of the play.

did happen, and to a family with links to some of the mightiest people in the land. The killer, Walter Calverley, had married Philippa Brooke in 1599. She was a member of the Brooke family, which included no less a person than Sir Robert Cecil; Philippa was Cecil's aunt. Cecil became Secretary of State in 1596, and held on to power for a considerable time by the standards of the Elizabethan period and was still a key man in James I's Government (he was called 'the little beagle' by the king).

Insanity in the Family

What actually happened that awful day in April 1605 we will almost certainly never know. Walter had been in severe trouble with his mounting debts; he had been selling off much of his extensive land in the East Riding, as well as property in Pudsey, Burley and Menston. In fact, the couple had been married for only a year when the new husband was imprisoned for debt and was very ill. His mother-in-law had described him as 'unstayed' (unstable) and there was a history of insanity in his family. His father, William, was undoubtedly a lunatic who remained a fervent Catholic at a time when that could have cost him his life. In 1569 the Catholics in the North had risen against the monarch and the reprisals when that failed were savage in the extreme. William senior was also imprisoned at one time in London for making speeches of a seditious nature in public. He died young, at the age of just 39. The man had massive fines imposed on him for absence from church, so the political and legal pressures were tight. It seems quite amazing that the Brookes allowed Walter Calverley's marriage into their ranks at all.

The pressures from debt, religious belief and those of marriage into a powerful family no doubt weighed heavily on Walter, and that spring he snapped. There had been a catalyst, since there had been a notable witch trial in the area just a month before he went into his rage. Locals had been spoken of with suspicion by their neighbours and it was all turning nasty.

A Man under Pressure

What was there left for Calverley and his sons? He must have thought that death would release the boys from a life of penury and suffering. To make matters worse (and here we must read between the lines) his own mother, Katherine, who had lands around Burton Agnes, was buying more land and her wealth grew. She had said that she was not intending to leave any of this wealth to her stressed and unbalanced son.

The details we have of what happened at the hall come from a pamphlet published just a few weeks after the murders. Strangely, other legal documentation has not survived, and that seems to be rather more than coincidence when we realise that the Brooke family was in bigger trouble: Lord Brooke was a friend of Sir Walter Raleigh, and he followed him into disgrace, being reprieved by James I in December 1603. Raleigh, shut in the Tower of London on a charge of treason, was executed in 1618. The new king was looking for a 'good press' on his arrival from the north, and Brooke's connections there may have saved him, whereas Raleigh had made enemies at court.

We rely for the narrative, then, on the pamphlet. This has Walter as a man under pressure from the start: a man ranting about his wife's infidelity. Then troubles come thick and fast, such as a report that his brother is in gaol, and that is the last straw for him. One poor son comes on stage with a whip and top and is promptly stabbed. Then he loses control totally and raves into his wife's room. In a desperate struggle as his wife tries to fight him off the children, Walter stabs the other boy and then his wife. She falls down wounded and Walter runs to find the other son, who is also wounded. The language is equal to any popular thriller:

'Husband: Comest thou between my fury to question me?

Servant: Were you the Devil I would hold you Sir.

Husband: Hold me? Presumption, I'll undo thee for it!

Servant: Sblood! You have undone us all, Sir.'

Retribution

Walter is finally tracked down after he has run away in a rage, then dragged before a magistrate and taken to Wakefield (not to York as there was a plague there at the time). But later he was moved to York and kept there until the next Assize. We know just two bare facts about the outcome. First, that Walter was pressed to death on 5 August, and buried on the same day; and second that he was buried in the grounds of St Mary's. We think immediately of the death of Margaret Clitherow when we think of pressing as a method of execution: slow and barbarous in the extreme. The prisoner would be naked under a board and then stones would be gradually placed on the board to crush him to death.

Walter's wife married again a few years later. She had three daughters, and she lived until 1613. Two entries in burial registers tell the hard facts of the Yorkshire tragedy. The first says simply, 'Calverley, St Wilfrid's 24 April 1605. Wllm and Walter, sons of Walter Calverley Esq.' The second is more explicit and powerful:

'York, St Mary's Castlegate 5 Aug. 1605

Walter Calverley executed for murthering unnaturally

Two of his own children the 23 April 1605

Was buried the said 5 August.'

A.C. Cawley, the literary scholar, points out the lingering fascination of the case. As he notes, Calverley's reasons for remaining mute at the trial 'are not clear at all.' Refusing to plead actually protected his land and stock, because the assets were left in a trust so that they would not be lost when the owner committed a felony. A felony entailed the loss of all possessions, as a rule, so people searched for ways around that problem. Maybe Walter was much more canny than he seemed, and in control in some ways. A simpler solution, as Cawley suggests, is that 'he may have been seeking the speediest way to end his life'. If so, then he certainly succeeded.

The text of *A Yorkshire Tragedy* lies on the bookshelves in the English Literature section of the university libraries, but beneath that academic exterior lies one of the worst, most heart-rending murders in the history of the county.

TWO

The Battle of Adwalton Moor

'The besieged at Bradford now found themselves
in a most pitiable plight'

William Scruton

During the course of the terrible English Civil Wars of 1641–52 Bradford experienced two attacks. The first happened in 1642 when the assaults led to a desperate fight in which the so-called Dead Lane was at the centre. On that occasion the hero was John Hodgson, whose tough defence meant that, as Scruton put it, 'If the Puritan cloth-workers of Bradford could pray and sing psalms, the cavaliers were not long in finding out that they could fight too.' In that assault, 800 Royalist soldiers had come to the town from Leeds, commanded by Sir William Saville. Cannon were positioned at Undercliffe, and then fighting began in the town itself.

The citizens were armed with anything they could use as a weapon, and it was a few days after this that Hodgson arrived. It was a case of hand-to-hand fighting and some Royalist officers were captured and killed. This fight has become known as the Battle of the Steeple, and it was particularly heartening as ordinary citizens had defeated troops and aristocrats.

There were threats from the Royalists to destroy the town; the alarm was great and Parliamentarian Bradford took measures to defend itself. On that first confrontation Hodgson had gathered men from Halifax to help their neighbours, and they did stalwart work. Obviously word spread to the King's men in the north, and the powerful Sir Thomas

Fairfax came to the town to offer help to the Parliamentarians. Hodgson stayed to serve with 'Black Tom' Fairfax and there was then a build-up to what was to be a more significant attack on the town.

The Earl of Newcastle and his Army

The Royalists had more manpower than Fairfax, and in June 1643 the Earl of Newcastle moved against the town with a force of 10,000 men. Fairfax went out to meet the enemy, and he had around 6,000 fewer men at his command. Newcastle would find himself besieged at York, but for now his star was in the ascendancy. The forces were to meet on Adwalton Moor, four miles from Bradford in the direction of Wakefield. It has not been written about very often and the action has been eclipsed by other events in the war, but Fairfax himself wrote an account of it in his *A Short Memorial of Northern Actions During the War There*. This covered the years of 1642 to 1644, and there is another account written by Thomas Stockdale. Stockdale was riding with Fairfax and he explained the composition of the Parliamentarian force very clearly.

Newcastle had heard of the advance against him, and moved his men from Howley forward to place them on high ground, while at the same time he dispersed men around the edge in a number of houses, as Stockdale wrote: 'Upon Atherton Moor they placed their ordnance and ordered their battalia, but they manned divers houses standing in the ground betwixt Bradford and Atherton Moor with musketeers, and sent out great parties Of horse and foot by the lanes and enclosed grounds to give us fight...'

The course of the battle has a familiar ring when we consider what tends to happen when forces of unequal number are ranged against each other. The Yorkshiremen were brave and resolute, attacking the forces in the lanes, and the 'forlorn hope' men did great work clearing the detachments of Royalists out of the buildings, but then the situation was that most of Fairfax's men were of course outnumbered while in a vulnerable position.

The Roundheads pushed too far against the larger force and began to feel the stress of losing men, especially as they were gradually fighting on a gradient, with the enemy cavalry above them. Newcastle's men had enough in reserve to encircle Fairfax's force. Fairfax wrote that he and his father, Ferdinando, worked hard to keep an enclosure and withstand charges; Fairfax himself commanded the strongest element of the force, the right wing, and Major General Clifford led the left wing.

Charge or Retreat?

Fairfax explained part of his failure in terms of misunderstandings, but there was also great bravery on the part of the Royalists. Colonel Skirton, called by Fairfax 'a wild and desperate man' led a charge against pikes and broke through, allowing more forces of Newcastle's to break through the gap and pursue. The route back to Bradford was blocked and the Royalists exploited their superior numbers in cavalry to charge and hit their enemy hard at the weakest points.

It seems as though the King's men considered a retreat at one point; this was after the solid impact of Clifford's charge from the left. At that vital point, when the tide could have turned either way, Skirton made his rash but successful charge.

So What Happened?

Most battles are very difficult to understand in relation to who moved where, when and why. But in the case of Adwalton, the accounts given by both sides differ so much that the truth is hard to find. Royalist writers claimed that the Bradford men were on the scene first and had chosen the battle site. They claimed that Fairfax's men chose exactly where they were to fight. The Royalist Henry Slingsby wrote what appears to be a clear account of events, concentrating on how the cavalry of his side turned the day their way: 'But seeing lieutenant-general King advance with all the horse that remained and wheeling about to get between the town and their forces, and also the colours advancing in a thick body up the hill...Stockdale stood at my Lord Fairfax's elbow, advised my Lord not to hazard the rest, seeing all was lost; but to shift for himself; so that they were totally routed.'

It was an important battle, because it opened up a vulnerable area of the North to Newcastle. From his strong position of power as he marched on to Bradford, comes the story of the Bolling Hall ghost, one of the most celebrated legends of the city.

Fairfax on the Run

Fairfax lived to fight another day. He had realised that he had to surrender Bradford, and that he must save himself for future work. He managed to escape to Leeds, but his wife, Lady Ann Vere, was captured and taken prisoner. She was taken at the place where the Cock and Bottle public house stood in the High Street. Newcastle let her go home in his own carriage.

Fairfax was to become commander-in-chief of Oliver Cromwell's New Model Army. He was voted in to that important role by 101 votes to 69. Fairfax was a dashing, dramatic figure; it was said that he won over his colleagues by sheer confidence and presence. One writer noted that in battle Fairfax was transformed 'out of his habitual silence into an angel' and Milton said that he conquered not the enemy alone but ambition. He had been nicknamed 'Black Tom' because of his Italianate looks and long dark hair.

After Adwalton he had to run and lick his wounds, waiting for a chance of revenge. It might be said that his men should not have taken the offensive but waited in Bradford, but the wisdom of hindsight is never any comfort and can never be called the right perspective, not even with the certainty of the best theorists. His attitude to Bradford he expressed in these words: 'The town is untenable, but for their good affection for us, deserving all we could hazard for them...'

The Apparition

Newcastle took Bradford, and one historian expressed the situation with the words, 'Oh what a night was that in which Bradford was taken! What weeping and wringing of hands!...None expected to live any longer than when the enemy came into the town...'

But then we have the story of the lady in white who reputedly saved Bradford from any intended horrible fate. Newcastle stayed at Bolling Hall and the story is that, while he was sleeping, the ghost of a white lady appeared to him and said, 'Pity poor Bradford!' as she pulled the bedclothes away from him. Newcastle was allegedly then convinced that he must indeed follow the pleas and he sent orders for Bradford to be spared. That did happen, and that is all that matters, whatever the truth of the tale. Some have even suggested that a Bradford lass dressed up and

Image of the *Pity poor Bradford* story.

PITY POOR BRADFORD

put on the act, in a desperate move to rattle the great man in his moment of triumph. Whatever the truth, the story has persisted and been embellished, and stands as a piece of famous local folklore.

Bradford in the Civil War

At the time of the battle, Bradford was of course supporting Parliament. The place suffered economically for that allegiance. Just as it was becoming a thriving community, with a good reputation for clothing of many kinds, it was hit hard. A Victorian historian gives some figures to reflect that decline, noting that births, marriages and deaths were, respectively, in 1639: 209, 61 and 183. The equivalent figures for the year 1659, not long after the wars, were 113, 38 and 117.

THREE

The Magistrate Turns Sleuth

'Throughout the eighteenth century, counterfeiting and clipping were among the commonest offences'

John Marsh

Before England had any kind of police force other than wardsmen and watchmen, it was very difficult to trap a felon and even more of a challenge to locate a network, ring or gang of villains working across the country. Yet that is what one Bradford magistrate did in the great age of the 'yellow clippings', when determined crooks clipped the King's coinage to melt down and make more money. They were risking the noose.

Popular history books and the media have given us a general picture of the 18th-century magistrate that tends to suggest an idle, over-fed and useless character, too keen to have his next meal, who fills the gaols just to maintain his quiet life. Perhaps this owes a lot to popular novels of the time, but documents do sometimes indicate that a magistrate did not stir from his favourite chair unless there was an extreme emergency such as a riot or imminent war.

Forgeries Galore

The years from the middle of the 18th century to the end of the 19th century were years in which forgery and counterfeiting of all varieties were widely practised. Not only were coins forged and clipped, but banknotes were also forged; in the first decades of that period, there were numerous regional banks issuing their own notes, in spite of the fact that we had had a Bank of England since 1689. Also, in other documentation such as bills of exchange and drafts, forgery was rife. The tendency was for criminals to work in networks and use local craftsmen for different skills, as required by particular activities. It was a tough job for the forces of law, trying to crack the wicked tricks and cons of these men.

Samuel Lister

There was at least one exception to the stereotype of the 18th-century magistrate, and it was in the Bradford and Halifax area between 1751 and 1769. This was Samuel Lister, a formidable man to have as an enemy and, unluckily for the men involved in the yellow trade of coining and clipping and in the risky activity of forgery at that time, he was more than capable of going out to make things happen, and playing detective when needed. Lister was based at Horton House and he had been trained as an attorney, spending 13 years in that profession. He had to suspend his legal work if and when he was needed to act as the magistrate.

There was a family tradition behind this; Lister's father had served on the bench for the West Riding and, as the area covering Bradford and Calderdale was vast, mostly wild and empty, and in the first stages of an industrial revolution, a magistrate was sure to be kept busy. Where there are rich and poor in close proximity, there will be much crime. At that time, the response to crime was repression: there were around 200 capital offences, and plenty of local lock-ups. Stocks and houses of correction kept the less serious offenders out of circulation for a while. In 1764, in the Halifax parish of Lister's area, there was most likely a population of approximately 40,000 and there was no magistrate in local residence when Lister stepped into the role. Bradford had three justices in the 1750s. We are dealing with a remarkable man here, one who was highly regarded by the Marquis of Rockingham, the outstanding legal figure for the West Riding.

Enter William Wilkins

Lister had plenty to occupy him when dealing with the activities of thieves and robbers, and in this work he averaged about 26 sittings each year; but it was in the coining circuit that he really came out from his usual role to become a detective, out to get his man. The man in question in his most important case was one William Wilkins, who had been arrested and brought to the court for not paying bills at various hostelries throughout the West Riding. He had been searched and interrogated and on his person were found letters, one with a Gloucester postmark, and more astonishingly, a promissory note for the huge sum of £1,100 – a massive fortune at the time.

Wilkins said that he was from a place called Painswick in Gloucestershire, but the letters and notes he had were not actually signed by anyone of note. They were more than likely to be forgeries and, if guilty, Wilkins would hang. But the problem was, how to prove that he was guilty? It was going to take extraordinary measures to achieve this, notably trying to communicate with the Painswick authorities, and this was something usually far too strenuous and time-consuming for your average magistrate to bother with. But not Samuel Lister though, for he was a determined man with a relish for such a daunting challenge.

Good Police Work

The first step was to enlist some qualified assistance, so he turned to a Leeds man, the Recorder Richard Wilson. At that time, a recorder was a barrister permitted to act as a Justice of the Peace at Quarter Sessions, so he certainly knew the law, and he knew the ways of criminals. The two men decided to keep Wilkins locked up while information was gathered; they put items in London newspapers and sent messages to Gloucester. They were pushed for time, as Wilkins was due to appear at the Lent Assizes in the South West very soon. He could have had friends there to stand bail as well, so they moved fast. This is where the alacrity of Lister in using the 'grapevine' around Bradford paid off, as one of his regular contacts knew of a West Country man visiting the town, a certain Walter Merrett. He advised Lister to write to a clothier at Uley near Painswick, to ascertain some information.

It was a triumph: 'Wilkins' was in fact Edward Wilson from Painswick who was wanted for forgery. Matters were soon finalised and in a short time Wilson was sent for trial at Gloucester on 20 March 1756. There he was sentenced to death.

Lister against the Yorkshire Coiners

Lister also began to act against the local clippers. This trade involved filing or clipping coins down to an acceptable weight for local use, and

The Old Cock, Halifax, where Hartley the coiner was arrested.

actually creating more coins from the clippings. It was very lucrative and very risky. The dangers were acute and it made criminals act with desperation and resolve, even to the extent of murder if they had to, as in the case of the killing of the excise man William Deighton in Halifax in 1769. But the Bradford men still acted against the coiners, perhaps urged on by this murder. It was no easy task to work against these rogues, though: the trade enjoyed considerable popular support. Lister was a part of the crusade against these coiners from the distant and inaccessible valleys towards Lancashire.

The best way to search out the men involved in coining was to employ *agents provocateurs*, men who would work their way into the confidence of the criminals and then betray them. Lister, together with John Hustler in Bradford, did this most successfully, their work leading to the arrest of two men on an inspector's evidence, and they were packed off to York Castle. Lister must have known the risks he was taking. Deighton had sent men to York Castle to await the noose, and he had paid for it with his life.

A Rare Achievement

Samuel Lister was indeed a remarkable man. He saw the magistracy as something opening up opportunities to act, not only on behalf of the civil order and law itself, but as a means of reinforcing the authority in economic and commercial contexts as well. The action against the 'yellow trade' was done partly because he had links with local industrialists and he represented their interests in protecting the value of coins in circulation. His principal biographer, John Styles, appropriately quotes Lister's own words as an explanation of his motives: 'I think it my duty not only as a magistrate but as a private person to do all that I am able to bring villains to justice.'

The battle against the forgers went on, and even as late as 1820 there was a ring of counterfeiters, a group linking Hull men with a gang in the West Midlands. It is interesting to note the similarity to the 'Wilkins' case. Clearly the criminal craftsmen were around Birmingham, and perhaps Yorkshire was perceived as distant and 'primitive' in terms of communication. How wrong they were in the case of detective Lister.

FOUR

Chartists and Rebels

'In 1837 O'Connor made up his mind that the real centre of popular agitation was to be found not in London, but in the factory districts of the north.'

G.D.H. Cole

In Beverley House of Correction in 1840 Robert Peddie, the Bradford Chartist, was starting his sentence of three years hard labour for his involvement in the Bradford uprising. He and other imprisoned Chartists complained that they were not common criminals but were 'political' and so should not have to work on the treadmill. They fought a losing battle, as the state saw them as very dangerous indeed, and they were to be crushed in the harsh prison regime of the 'Silent System' in which every day was hard work, with no association and meagre food. Such was the fear instilled by the Chartism movement across the country in the 1830s and 1840s, and Bradford was very much a focal point of that movement.

The Chartists were political activists who emerged after the disappointments of the 1832 Reform Act. Although that legislation did widen the franchise, it still excluded a very large number of people from the vote, most markedly the working people, from labourers to artisans. Linked with the ideals of the early trade unions and the radical clubs, the movement was seen by the state as a subversive activity and they watched as it gathered massive support and spread to many parts of England and Wales.

The Chartist programme was a series of political demands; they compiled a six-point charter, demanding universal suffrage, annual parliaments, vote by secret ballot, the abolition of the property qualification for MPs, payment of MPs and more fair and equal electoral districts.

In the north, particular local leaders emerged, along with nationally renowned figures such as the Irishman Feargus O'Connor, who started the influential radical newspaper *The Northern Star* and later came to believe in 'physical force' Chartism – a path that led to large-scale trouble.

Events in Bradford

In 1840 W.J. Williams produced a report on prisoners in York Castle who had taken part in the Chartist rising. One man, Emanuel Hutton, aged 28, had been sentenced to 18 months of hard labour in Wakefield gaol. He was a wool comber, and his condition was described as 'much distressed.' Williams reported that Hutton was aware that there had been a movement known as 'physical force' Chartism, and it seems that he read the radical newspapers and had been on the margin of events.

The prisoner told how he joined a crowd. Not really knowing what was happening, he was led into trouble: 'I saw a man who bade me go into the market place with them – one gave me a gun.' The hard fact is that in the year building up to the risings in South Wales and then in Lancashire and Yorkshire at this time, many of the plans conceived had involved plans to murder police constables. On Woodhouse Moor in nearby Leeds, Feargus O'Connor had been drilling his forces. It was a national emergency, all based on the widespread political exclusion of working men. Other discontents were compounding their problems: the high cost of food, long hours of labour for poor pay, and the excess of the population after a massive drift into the new towns from rural work. O'Connor had been a well-known figure in this context around Yorkshire at the time, mainly due to his newspaper but also for his power as a public speaker.

Confrontation and Anger

The Bradford wool combers were among those workers who were suffering from the deprivations of the harsh times, and they were therefore fertile ground for the demagogues, and of course for those who thought violence was the best way to achieve results.

In 1839 the wide open space of Hartshead Moor, or Peep Green as it then was, became the scene of one of the largest Chartist rallies of all time. The area was like a fair, with over 100 huts in place for the sale of food and drink. Some said that half a million people had turned up, but a more realistic figure is perhaps 200,000. This was on 18 October, and O'Connor was there, talking about the death of tyrants; another leader, Bussey, insisted that the best thing that Bradford men could do was buy guns. Hartshead had been in use before, back in May 1837 when it staged a Poor Law meeting. It was fast becoming a spot in Bradford with a disturbing reputation in the eyes of the local agencies of law.

Men did listen to Bussey, and they went to arm themselves. Justices of the Peace started taking depositions from shop-keepers who had had visits from desperate men bent on using firearms. William Egan, a Bradford gunsmith, recalled how he had had visits from such locals. He stated after the events, as he stood as a witness, '...a person whom I did not know and who appeared to be in the capacity of a labourer called at my shop and asked me if I had any guns and bayonets by me, to which I answered that I had not.' Pressure was being exerted; men were desperate to arm and to take on the local authority. Egan said that in one period of about 10 days he had 'been applied to in order to alter muskets which have been brought to me without the stocks.'

Spies in the Town

The town's hand-loom weavers had a very hard time, and there were plenty of them involved in the Chartist rising. Not only were they extremely poor, but they also had had to cope with all the diseases of poverty and deprivation: cholera, smallpox, typhus and other similar maladies. Infant mortality was the most poignant aspect of these impoverished lifestyles: in 1842 around 1,500 children under five years of age died in the town and surrounding parts of the borough.

When the desperate men put their militancy into action, hands grasping swords and guns, the Government had a tried and tested method of counterattack – the use of spies. These *agents provocateurs* infiltrated the radicals. They became big news as well: the Leeds newspaper owner, Edward Baines, exposed the most infamous of them, one 'Oliver'. He was also written about by one of the most celebrated working-class radicals, Samuel Bamford, the Lancashire man.

In Bradford, James Harrison was an active Government spy and in December 1839 he gave an account of what was going on among the extremists. He had been to a meeting at the Queen's Head, four miles from the city centre, and there he heard that there were around 260 men armed and ready to make trouble. There was also a London Chartist at this meeting, and Harrison must have been worried that he would be uncovered. He recalled: 'In the bar there was this delegate, George Flinn, two men from the Queen's Head and myself. The man from London looked earnestly at me and asked Flinn if he knew me. Flinn said he had known me for three years and I was as good as any man in the room...' How wrong can a man be? But it was a perilous life for these Government men, as they must have suspected that their fate would have been a brutal death if they were found out.

The magistrates were frightened, and wrote to the Home Secretary expressing their concerns. These were E.C. Lister of Manningham, Matthew Thompson, H.W. Hird and W.R. Stansfield. They wrote about 'violent harangues of evil disposed and Revolutionary speakers'. And they felt that 'some violent outrage' was about to take place. According to one memoir, admittedly by O'Connor who is not always trustworthy in these matters, it was a Bradford man who organised a nationwide rising at that time. He said it was Peter Bussey, a Bradford innkeeper, who was responsible, stating 'This fellow got up several committees, to be held in different parts of the country, to establish the best means for getting up a revolution...'

1840 – the Debacle

The leader of the abortive revolt was Robert Peddie, and a parallel rising was to take place in Sheffield, with whom the Bradford men had good relations. Peddie's narrative explains most things that took place. The plans of Peddie and his peers must have been terrifying to Bradford, which then had a population of 66,000 and a police force of half a dozen men. There was no real police force outside London (the Municipal Corporations Act of 1835 had started borough forces, but they were slow in formation), and Peel's Police Act establishing the metropolitan force had only been in action for 11 years. It is no wonder that localities were still relying on the army in these situations, so naturally a group of ordinary labouring men would have no chance of success against a militia force, and this was the case with Peddie's plans. James Harrison outlined Peddie's notions of a co-ordinated revolt, involving miners from further afield as well as the Bradford people. Harrison met with a gang of insurgents at the Junction Tavern on Leeds New Road, and the plan was to go to Leeds and set fire to the militia magazine. Peddie's talk certainly included the desire to achieve the Chartists' aims, but there was another agenda, feeding other criminal discontents as well.

Everything was nipped in the bud, however, as the plans and leaders were known. Major General Charles Napier was given command of what was then called the Northern District in 1839. He soon had men billeted around the West Riding conurbation – for instance 42 men in Halifax in just as many houses, and altogether in Yorkshire he had 1,000 troops. He had to act quickly; very extreme things were happening, such as a book in circulation in Halifax about facing barricades and how to face cavalry with a pike.

Prison and Failure

Peddie was given a three-year sentence after the Chartist trials of 1840. His Sheffield counterpart, Martin, was sent to distant Northallerton to waste away on the treadmill. As for O'Connor, who had figured at a national level, his trial was very high profile and lasted for several weeks. In the end no policemen were killed in the streets, but that would not be long in coming, as Chartism was to last until the final failure of 1848. D.G. Wright has noted that Peddie's colourful radical career made him enemies on his side of the law as well. Wright says that at one point, 'The Scots Chartists decided they had had enough of this wilful, self-centred and histrionic man.'

The national plans were then uncovered and Chartist

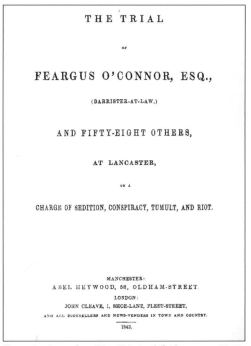

THE TRIAL

OF

FEARGUS O'CONNOR, ESQ.,

(BARRISTER-AT-LAW,)

AND FIFTY-EIGHT OTHERS,

AT LANCASTER,

ON A

CHARGE OF SEDITION, CONSPIRACY, TUMULT, AND RIOT.

MANCHESTER:
ABEL HEYWOOD, 58, OLDHAM-STREET.
LONDON:
JOHN CLEAVE, 1, SHOE-LANE, FLEET-STREET,
AND ALL BOOKSELLERS AND NEWS-VENDERS IN TOWN AND COUNTRY.
1843.

Frontispiece for *The Trial of O'Connor,* 1843.

Baron Rolfe, who tried O'Connor.

connections were seen and understood by all involved. The historian, Mark Hovell, summarised this situation in his 1943 study of the movement: 'About the same time the Bradford magistrates reported secret proceedings. They managed to corrupt a Chartist, and obtained information of the intended rising. On December 17 they received a long report... The rising was to take place on the 27th. A secret convention would meet in London on the 19th and give the signal. There had been a meeting in Manchester the previous week...The soldiery were to be harassed by systematic incendiarism...'

It is when we read details such as this that we begin to understand the reactions of the Government; these plans were indeed subversion and revolt of the most terrifying kind.

But for the Bradford radicals it all ended in the gaol and the treadmill, eating porridge and listening to seemingly endless sermons about the possibility of redemption. The only redemption they wanted was to be treated like proper and respected citizens of their country, men allowed to vote on who should represent their wishes and aspirations.

FIVE

Tales of Methodists, from Nelson to Lax

'John Wesley was not the founder of Bradford Methodism:
He reaped where others had sown.'

Simon Valentine

John Wesley did preach in Bradford – at Little Horton Hall and at Sticker Lane, being there in 1744, just six years after his enlightenment in Aldersgate, London, and the subsequent birth of Methodism. But, as Simon Valentine has pointed out, Bradford really owes the beginnings of Methodism in its streets and homes to stonemason John Nelson, who was also converted in London.

John Nelson: 'a high spirit and a brave heart…'
In 1741 Nelson came back to Bradford and spent time with the Moravians, but then he went his own way and washed up on the shores of Wesleyan thought, beginning to hold small meetings at his own home in Birstall. According to the main tradition, the first Methodist meeting was held by Nelson at the door of a dungeon – that in Ivegate. He ended up there because his enemies wanted him out of the way, and the quickest method of achieving that was to have him enlisted in the army. But friends interceded and he was to be sent to York instead; he was placed in Ivegate on the way and there the meeting was held, as he describes in his journal: '…several of the people came to the dungeon door and brought me some candles, and put me some meat and water in through the hole of the door. When I had eaten and drank I gave God thanks and we sang hymns almost all night, they without and I within.'

John Nelson in the Bradford dungeon. (from Scruton's *Pen and Pencil Sketches of Old Bradford*, 1889)

Although someone offered bail for Nelson, it was not accepted and he remained in gaol for some months. One view is that the vicar of Birstall was responsible for this persecution of a man who was described by the poet Robert Southey as a man with 'a high spirit and as brave a heart as ever Englishman was blessed with'.

He was taken to Leeds and finally, after the intervention of the Countess of Huntingdon, he was released and returned home. By 1747 the first Methodist society was formed in Bradford and a leading light was Thomas Mitchell, who had been a soldier. He wrote about Wesley's visit in that year, and in a rather strange way: 'He joined several of us together in a class which met about a mile from the town. But all of them fell back and left me alone; yet afterwards some of them returned.'

As for Nelson, he died in Leeds on 18 July 1774, after being ill for just 90 minutes. He was buried in Birstall churchyard, with his wife Martha, who died just two months after him, with this for an inscription:

'While we on earth had our abode,
We both agreed to serve the Lord;
And He was pleased, as you may see,
By death not long us parted be;
Then He required the breath he gave,

And now we lie both in one grave,
Until again He us restore,
A life to live, and die no more.'

As his body was carried through Leeds on the way to Birstall, it was attended by thousands, either singing or weeping, as a magazine of the time reported.

Grimshaw

There was also a preacher named John Bennet who formed a society at Heaton in 1744 and Bennet's writings refer to preaching at various places around the town, including Shelf and Manningham. But William Grimshaw, firebrand of Haworth and inspiration for the character of Joseph in Emily Brontë's *Wuthering Heights*, takes centre stage when we consider the Methodists of Bradford. He was perpetual curate of Haworth, but had a group of preachers around him who toured the area, speaking in the open air most of the time.

Elizabeth Gaskell, in her *Life of Charlotte Brontë*, recounts the story of his enlightenment, an event supposedly dated to one Sunday in September

The Wesley family home, Epworth.

1744: 'As he went out, he spoke to the congregation, and told them not to disperse, as he had something to say to them and would return presently. He was taken to the clerk's house and again became insensible. His servant rubbed him to restore the circulation and when he was brought to himself he "seemed in great rapture" and the first words he uttered were, "I have had a glorious vision from the third heaven..."'

It was said that Grimshaw's ancestors claimed to be dragon slayers at a place called Blackburn Wood; he certainly had an extraordinary charisma and feared nothing. He became a close friend of John Wesley himself and the two of them used to travel into Keighley together to try to convert some of the most recalcitrant citizens. But on one occasion a mob assailed them, and the pair took shelter in a private house while the mob outside demanded that they leave town.

Grimshaw's character and approach to preaching is best illustrated by his famous line, 'If ye will go to hell, you shall go to hell with the sound of the gospel in your lugs!'

The Cock Pit and the Octagon Chapel

By 1756 there had been an increase in Methodist numbers and fervour, and a base was needed in the town. This was a large room in a place called the Bradford Cock Pit. The historian Scruton describes the spot as a den of iniquity: '...the place where Wesley, Whitfield and Grimshaw were wont to address multitudes of anxious hearers had but recently been the gathering place of disreputable gamblers and black-legs who revelled in such brutal sports as cock-fighting and bull-baiting...It would, perhaps, be difficult to find another spot that has been put to so many base uses as this old building.'

Sketches of the Cock Pit show clearly the steps from the top of which Wesley would preach; but through modern eyes we have to say that it was not a wise choice, as it was or had been the same place from which various more questionable and borderline religious characters had operated, including the infamous eccentric Mr Wroe from Bowling, who was the son of a worsted manufacturer but who did not follow his father's occupation. He acquired a religious mania after suffering a fierce infection, saying that he could see visions and dreams. He claimed to have visits from angels and was sure that he had a special mission on earth, sent by God.

The Wesley memorial, Epworth.

The Cock Pit had been many things: at one time it was a billet for troops, and then a court house. It had also been a warehouse and a school, but when it became a room for Methodist meetings it attracted more attention, and Wesley himself has left an account in his journals: 'Thursday, May 12th. The latter end of the week I spent in Bradford. Sunday 15 at 5 the house contained the congregation, but at eight they covered the Plain adjoining to it. The sun was hot till the clouds interposed; it was a Solemn and comfortable season.' (The plain was land near the Cock Pit and leading to a beck at the far end).

Eventually a better location was needed and the Octagon chapel was built. This was in Horton Road, and cost almost £1,000 by the time of the grand opening on 27 July 1776. Wesley wrote that it was 54sq ft, 'the largest octagon we have in England'. Sadly, it was to last only 40 years, as the walls were unsafe.

The 19th century

By 1825 Bradford had the Eastbrook Chapel and, following that came the Kirkgate Chapel, but by 1890, when Scruton wrote his history, he could say that in addition, 'in the district and outlying villages, many fine and spacious buildings have been reared in order to keep pace with the large and ever-increasing population'. These included the White Abbey Chapel at Manningham (1838) and the chapel at Allerton designed by Herbert Issitt (1886).

The Primitive Methodists and the New Connexion were present by 1824 and 1839 respectively. When the *Bradford Observer* did a survey in 1881 it found that just over a quarter of the population of 194,000 were regular worshippers, and the Methodists were still the most populous of the many Non-conformist groups in the town.

Towards the end of the century there were notable characters in the Methodist ranks, men like H.M. Nield, who wanted to increase the strength of the gospel argumentation expressed to the ordinary citizen. He gave lectures especially for the working man and invited people to attend his debates on important issues and concepts. Simon Valentine tells the story of Nield entitling one event 'What'll Win' – on the topic of gambling. Someone sent him a card with the name of a winner of a forthcoming race, and when he read it out the tip had come off. People's interest in Mr Nield increased amazingly after that.

Lax and Hird

These two names represent something interesting in the history of Methodism. First, William Lax, who was to become famous later in his life as 'Lax of Poplar' following his work with the poor in the Docklands area of east London, gave a sermon at St George's Hall in 1896 when he was assigned to a ministry in Bradford, and although he had the seemingly important role of being District Missionary to Halifax and Bradford he found himself sharing the stage with the charismatic Hugh Price Hughes at the Hall in 1897. Law wrote: 'I had never seen Hughes before. That tall, striking figure, with slightly greying hair, the close-bearded, almost terrifyingly fierce face, simply held me. He carried himself with a distinguished, aristocratic air...When he rose to speak, marvel followed marvel...It was overwhelming. I had heard great speaking before, but never had I seen an audience mastered and driven where one man wanted it to go, and I saw it then...'

Lax of Poplar. (from *Lax his book*, 1938)

A more humorous side of Methodism: letter concerning a father's study group, 1920s.

Lax was asked to go to London to be assistant to Price Hughes, and his Bradford work ended. He recalls going back to his lodgings in West Bowling, thinking of Bradford as the place where his life's work was formed.

On the other hand, in alderman Horace Hird we have a man who made Methodism a cause, not simply of faith, but of the collector's preoccupation. He was born in 1900 into a steeplejack business and left school at 13 to follow the family business, staying with the firm all his life until it ceased trading in 1964. Horace Hird was a member of the Victoria Hall mission in Otley Road Methodist Circuit and later he was active in the Frizinghall Methodist Church.

Later, Hird became Lord Mayor and also wrote on the history of local government in Bradford. But it is in his persona as an antiquary that we have his importance in a context other than his practical faith and good work: he collected Wesleyana, and over a period of 30 years. After his death in 1973, his collection was left to the church and later came into the ownership of the Methodist Church Archives.

The Hird collection includes earthenware, portraits, figures, ceramics and prints. In an unusual way, it is in these two men that we see another perspective on Methodism: one represents that need for the conviction given by a true calling to be in the 'church militant', while the latter shows us that everyday good works and an imaginative adherence to the icons and meanings of a religion can be as inspiring as a theoretical line of thought. In both instances Bradford provided the impetus for a life of devotion and good works.

SIX

The Year of Garrotters and Robbers

1862

'The streets were fearful places, with killers sensed at every corner...'

Annual Register

Until 17 July 1862 there had been only 15 robberies with violence in the city of London. But then a Member of Parliament, one Hugh Pilkington, was 'garrotted' in Pall Mall. A new and terrifying crime against the person had been noted.

In its chronicle of November 1862 the *Annual Register* reported that there had been a 'garrotte terrorism' in London and in the provinces that year. The word 'garrotte' was beginning to strike terror into ordinary people and newspapers were selling on headlines about this new version of street robbery. The report expresses the crime in this way: 'For some years past there have been occasional instances of "garrotte robberies" – a method of highway plunder, which consists in one ruffian seizing an unsuspecting traveller by the neck and crushing in his throat, while another simultaneously rifles his pocket; the scoundrels then decamp, leaving their victim on the ground writhing in agony...'

The popular magazine *Punch* covered the menace with its usual acuteness and dash; one cartoon shows some middle-class theatre-goers venturing out

THE GAROTTER'S FRIEND
'Let go, Bill, can't yer it's our kind non-interfering friend, Sir George Grey!!!'

Cartoon about the garrotting menace. *(Punch)*

into the streets with a platoon of soldiers guarding them. It was nothing less than a reign of terror and it gradually became much more widespread than simply London's theatreland.

Moral Panic

This 'modern peril of the streets' was first described graphically as 'putting the hug on' and it had its own jargon, the gang members having particular roles. First, the man called the *front stall*, a look-out, then the *back stall* who was going to grab the booty, and finally the *nasty man* who would move in from behind to take the victim's throat. At the time it was seen as a variety of crime that was somehow not 'British' and journalists tried to blame it on foreigners. It was often written about in terms linked to activities by Italian mobs. But soon it was realised that this heinous crime was becoming a speciality of the new criminal underclass of the expanding towns across Victorian England.

The terror even entered the realms of popular song, with lines such as:

'A gentleman's walking, perchance with a crutch
he'll suddenly stagger and totter;
don't think that the gentleman's taken too much
he's unluckily met a garrotter...'

In the provinces the new crime began to take a hold towards the late summer of the year. 1862 was destined to become a proper *annus horribilis* for good people on the city streets, and northern towns were no exception. In Sheffield, one of the first notorious garrotters outside London was Edward Hall, a man who was apprehended after a desperate struggle with police. It was reported at the time that he was 'the leader of a gang of ruffians who garrotted and nearly murdered Mr Burnby, Earl

Fitzwilliam's coal agent'. He was cornered and surrounded, then jumped from a high window in his home in Sheffield to escape. But in Birmingham he was grabbed and almost killed by a huge police officer who punched the villain relentlessly until he gave in.

A Problem for the Bradford Police

In Bradford, the chief police officer, Frederick Granhan, was about to be busy with this new type of robbery and his constables' truncheons were going to be needed more than ever.

Characters like Hall began to appear in other parts of Yorkshire, and Bradford began to have its share of nasty street attacks by September that year. The streets of the city and the suburbs were indeed perilous at this time. A man was severely bitten by a dog in Grafton Street, and he almost had to have his leg amputated. A fishmonger in Keighley was robbed in broad daylight on his way back from a lunchtime tipple.

A more serious attack took place at Jerusalem in Thornton, where Joe Savile was attacked and robbed by two desperadoes who came across their victim at Well Heads. The attackers, James Jennings and William Shaw, showed no mercy; Jennings held the man's legs tight while Shaw grabbed his neck, then they ripped his coat off and somehow he fought free. As the poor man ran off, the robbers shouted that they would catch him and 'kill him off'. Amazingly, though, the accused were acquitted because of a lack of any clear accounts by witnesses.

Garrotter gangs were not so lucky, and the full weight of the law fell on them. William Holes and James Lynas were in court for their garrotte attack on William Dawson late on a Saturday night in Market Street. Dawson, an engine tender, yelled for the police to help and an officer came to the scene to see the two robbers running away down Kirkgate. Holmes was trapped in an alley. Lynas was taken in Collier Gate by a detective called Milnes. They had taken a few shillings and a silk handkerchief. At York Assizes they were to pay dearly for that attack, with a long prison sentence and hard labour waiting for them.

Lockwood and Murphy

In Calverley, on the moor, a Mr Summerscales was having his constitutional walk when he was set upon by two thugs called Elvidge and Hainsworth. They had used the established methods of one man behind to choke the victim while the other approached face to face, and they had taken his silver watch. But on this occasion, the victim could not positively identify the men and they lived to attack again.

Two hardened toughs called Lockwood and Murphy were one of the most successful garrotting teams around Leeds and Bradford, and they became adept at the atrocious business. They had a cover as street hawkers, one selling oysters and the other nuts. They trod the streets around the whole conurbation, and were finally tracked down after an attack in Hunslet, though they had been active in Armley and Bingley. Murphy was the 'nasty man' and appears to have been extremely threatening and dangerous. It is not difficult to see how this crime would catch on in the criminal ranks; it reached the proportions of being a 'glamour' offence in that it took skill, a brazen attitude and a total lack of fear. Lockwood and Murphy almost beat their last victim to death, and they took a trip to York Assizes where they were due to suffer physical punishment and years inside.

The press began to speculate about how the most likely recruits to the garrotting craze were 'ticket-of-leave' men. These were convicts whose terms of sentence had been lifted after good behaviour so that they could go into society to work, though they were required to attend musters, just as today we have a licence system in the current penal code. A ticket could be granted after the prisoner had served at least three years. Penal servitude had replaced the use of the prison hulks in the Thames estuary after 1853, and men who had only served three years of a seven-year sentence could be released under this scheme. The popular journals enjoyed creating this moral panic, making their readers envisage the local streets filling up with desperate and hardened criminals waiting to strangle them as they strolled to the Sunday bandstand concert.

The Law Steps In

All this led to the passing of the Garrotter's Act of 1863. In some quarters people raised a glass to the villains because their actions had introduced extreme and repressive punishments back into criminal law. In Bradford, the vogue had been just a small part of the life of a very violent and brutal community. One way of seeing this is to note that, while thugs were robbing in the dark streets, hundreds of men were gathering to watch bare-knuckle fighting, as they did at Cottingley Cliffs when Laverty and Curlly fought on a Monday morning in this violent year. Two officers found the men fighting 'near the bottom of a small secluded nook near Cottingley Moor, the ground around rising up in the form of an amphitheatre'. There were 600 people in the crowd, and the boxers were fighting for a prize of £10.

Everything about the city at this time suggests a community on the edge of reason and order. The women's refuge had hundreds of clients and even the traditional mummers' plays turned violent when fists flew on the doorsteps of good, honest people as the mummers' demands for cash grew too impertinent. There was even a minor scandal when some mill owners found themselves in the dock at the Borough Court. But at least there was no violence there – Thomas and Jeremiah Hall of Shipley had merely stolen £100 in a warehouse scam.

The year 1862 was a year of living dangerously in most English cities. In London street crime was obviously at a peak of atrocious violence, but the north was certainly not exempt from this 'new crime.' As so often, *Punch* saw the heart of the matter, and in their cartoon 'Jones is not afraid of his shadow' they summed up the nature of this particular fear. The little man with top hat and umbrella sees the giant shadow of a garrotter with a huge club on a wall as he walks along. But the good citizen in the picture, ironically, carries a revolver.

SEVEN

Charles Forshaw: Great Anthologist

'...and with sweet song soothe sorrow's sordid sting'.

Cliffe Castle by Charles Forshaw

Charles H. Forshaw. (*Yorkshire Notes and Queries*, 1905)

The author of the above alliterative line was a dentist with a penchant for verses. We may smile as we read now, but at the time anthologies were very popular and Charles just loved compiling them.

Charles Forshaw is remembered by few Yorkshire people today, and those who are familiar with his writings will know him as an anthologist of Yorkshire poetry rather than a poet. He was a dental surgeon in professional life in Bradford, but his love of poetry and local history led him to produce a vast amount of literature on Yorkshire and Yorkshire writers.

He was not a Yorkshireman, however, as he was born in Bilsdon, Staffordshire, on 23 January 1863. He studied chemistry and dentistry and became a Doctor of Dental Surgery in 1885. During his time as a dentist he received many honours, including an honorary LLD from Tusculum University, Tennessee, and an MD from Chicago National Medical University. He also wrote papers on the use of cocaine and on the microscopic structure of teeth. His early biographer, J.G. Gibson, collected all the facts about the honours conferred on Forshaw and the statistics of his literary career. Gibson says that, 'He has today (1908) written over one thousand biographies of poets and poetasters...fifty publications have issued from his pen...he has contributed verses to more than 5,000 journals and newspapers...'

Anthologies on Victorian Themes

What Forshaw wanted to do was collect poetry and fill books with it. He edited 16 collections of poetry of various kinds, mostly occasional poems or Yorkshire poetry. His love for the collection of a wide assortment of poems on a set theme, for instance, was always with him, along with poems of place and belonging. He collected anthologies of monodies on the deaths of Queen Victoria, W.E. Gladstone, Sir Henry Irving and many others. In the lists of his publications there are also such collections as *One Hundred of the Best Poems of the European War, by Poets of the Empire* and *Poetical Tributes on the Loss of the RMS* Titanic.

Forshaw's writings, or collections of other people's writings, are prodigious in number; yet, for all his interest in poetry, there is one sphere in which his work will always be useful and interesting – that is his interest in Yorkshire literature. In his lecture, *Some Yorkshire Poets* (1910), a poetry recital interspersed with a few biographical remarks, he gives some account of his work as an anthologist: 'In the course of issuing my collections of Yorkshire poetry I have come across upwards of two thousand Yorkshiremen who have written poetry...I have known of the millionaire Yorkshire poet – only one instance though – and I have known of poets who have died in the workhouses and prisons – all Yorkshiremen bear in mind – four of them were appointed Poet Laureate.'

The Antiquary

Above all else, Forshaw was an antiquary, a compulsive collector, but his importance does not end there. He did produce some work of literary value and, although he published half a dozen books of his own, the works of value are the prose writings. His lecture, mentioned above, is a valuable source-book for anyone interested in Victorian literature, but his best-known work is in *John Hartley: Poet and Author*, and his collections of Yorkshire poets with introductions in *Poets of Keighley, Bingley and Haworth* (1891), which includes examples from the work of John Nicholson the Airedale Poet and Patrick Brontë.

In his essay on John Hartley, the celebrated founder of the *Clock Almanac* and author of *Yorkshire Ditties*, there are fine passages of lively prose, as for instance in this account of Hartley giving a lecture in Quebec: 'The streets became rivers and traffic was stopped. One solitary individual managed to reach the hall in some way, and our Hartley waited patiently but in vain for an audience, but no one appeared! He was not to be deterred, however, and punctually made his appearance on the platform and went through one hour and a half's entertainment to his audience of ONE.'

This work on Hartley is short, but it gives us the character of the famous dialect writer and performer perfectly. At the end of the essay there is a subscription list applying for a Civil List pension for Hartley, which includes the names of people famous in literary history, such as Joseph Wright the scholar and W.S. Baring-Gould, the author of *Onward Christian Soldiers* and curate of Horbury. Forshaw himself subscribed of course, and the warmth of his essay on Hartley suggests that the wealthy Bradford dentist probably used all his influence to help Hartley in his old age.

Welsh Bard and other Honours

Throughout his writing career, Forshaw went on producing poems and compiling anthologies with admirable energy, and it seems a little sad that today his efforts have been largely forgotten. Yet in his own day he was immensely successful, becoming a Fellow of the Royal Society of Literature and Fellow of the Royal Historical Society. He was also a founder-member of the Brontë Society and the Thoresby Society. Today we might describe him as a 'dilettante', but linked to that was his role of committee man – maybe even a 'mover and shaker' in his own circumscribed world of letters.

All accounts of him suggest a really full life, with even a touch of romance and fantasy. Much of his spare time (when not pulling teeth or gathering poems) was spent in giving lectures, editing anthologies and journals such as *Yorkshire Notes and Queries*, but there were times when he entered an entirely different world. In the Coronation year of Edward VII for instance, Forshaw was made 'King's messenger' and chosen to deliver a message from the King to the people of St Kilda. Naturally, on his return, out came pen and paper and he produced a history of St Kilda – 'for the young princes', he said.

An even more incongruous event took place in 1904, for he was made, of all things, a Welsh Bard that year at the *Gorsedd*. He was given the bardic name of *Siarl Efrog,* which means 'Charles of York' and, as if this honour was not enough, he became Chevalier of the Order of Duty in France as well.

Who else could claim the title of true Yorkshireman ahead of this colourful and eccentric character? It seems strange that a man with so many academic honours did not produce a major work of criticism, but his work in Bradford certainly brought him fame in his time and place. He wished to be recognised above all as a poet and he kept on writing poetry, but it has little worth and has been largely forgotten. He had a clumsiness that he seemed not to be aware of, as in:

'Ye confused coronets of celebrated grace
That brightly gilt the arching dome of heaven.'

In his poem *To the Stars* and in his poem *To the London Fog* we have the lines,

'Men more like goblins, ghastly, gaunt and grim,
Enshrouded and enveloped 'mid its maze.'

Few people will find satisfaction in these today, but maybe he should have tried to express himself in local dialect.

Yorkshire Notes and Queries

It could be argued that Forshaw really came into his natural role when he edited the antiquarian and historical magazine *Yorkshire Notes and Queries* in the years around the end of the 19th century, and into the Edwardian period. This was a fascinating periodical concerned with all things Yorkshire, allowing correspondents to write and ask about

Front page of *Yorkshire Notes and Queries* for 1906.

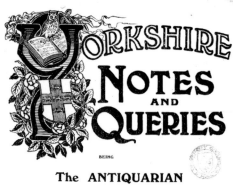

milestones, churches, coats of arms and famous soldiers or churchmen. In short, it was about the byways of the experience of living in Yorkshire through the centuries.

Perhaps Forshaw did not realise the importance of what he was doing for future folklorists and social historians of Bradford and related places. For instance, in one issue a discussion of the tradition of selling a wife filled a page, including an account from Bradford in 1858 when a man put his wife up for sale in a beer shop in Little Horton. That note provoked a list of other instances of that kind of event (as found most famously in Thomas Hardy's novel *The Mayor of Casterbridge*) with stories from Hull and elsewhere.

The journal is an absorbing read and succeeds in the way that mixtures of odd and surprising information still do today. Forshaw had found his metier in that work, and it was very successful around the county.

No doubt Charles Forshaw will be remembered as the author of source-books for writers on Yorkshire history, and the members of the Yorkshire Dialect and Folklore societies will meet his name in their researches. His writings give us not only an opening into Victorian Bradford, but in a wider sense they shine a light into the more obscure corners of the Victorian frame of mind.

EIGHT

Bradford Businessmen in Victorian Years

'In taking a bird's eye view of the colossal concerns of the adjacent town of Bradford...there are at least four remarkable establishments which stand boldly forward in the commercial horizon.'

James Burnley

James Burnley was thinking of the truly giant concerns of the town: those linked to the names of Lister, Holden, Salt and John Foster. But there were many others with all kinds of goods and services on offer as the town became a modern city. By the last few decades of the 19th century, handbooks, gazetteers and biographies celebrated the commercial genius of the Bradford men of business. The following is merely a small selection of some of these Victorian firms, some huge and some quite modest, yet still remarkable.

Daniel Illingworth
Whetley Mills, the home of the Illingworth empire, covered over eight acres of ground simply for the buildings, with a further floorage area of five acres. The illustration reproduced here shows that these mills were indeed composite and self-sufficient worlds within the city.

The Illingworth business in the worsted industry arrived on the industrial scene in the first years of the 19th century, founded by Miles

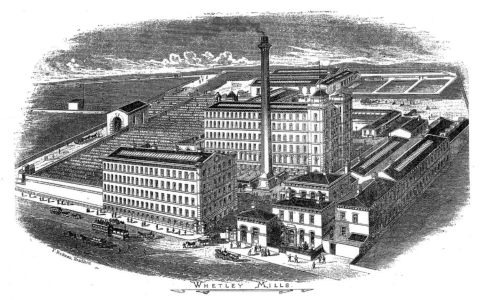

Illingworth's Mills, *c.*1890.

and Daniel Illingworth at Prospect Mill on Wakefield Road. They were then joined by a Mr Murgatroyd and moved to Hope Street in 1825. As expansion continued, the Illingworths rented Union Mill and by 1837 the family partnership was dissolved and Daniel carried on alone. He built some mills at Tetley Street, where the new Cornish boilers were put in place, such was the man's enterprise and sense of business adventure.

The new mills opened in 1838, well built with the local stone, and such was the Illingworth name and establishment by the end of the century that a celebratory publication gave this description of their impressive plant and efficiency: 'The spinning machinery is driven by a mammoth Corliss engine acting as an independent motor, while a third engine of the same type drives the preparing machinery. Steam is generated by a set of six 8 feet by 30 feet Beesley's boilers, fitted with Proctor's patent stoker. In the spinning industry, Illingworth's have always been in the van of progress...'

The last sentence could be seen as an understatement. Alfred and Henry Illingworth took over from Daniel and while Henry managed the mills, Henry bought wool and yarn. It proved to be a winning combination; the expansion eventually led to Whetley Mills being created in 1865, and a contemporary writer noted that they were 'among the largest and most perfectly organised establishment of the Bradford spinning industry.'

As usual, the Illingworths were far more than businessmen; Henry was a Justice of the Peace for the area, and Alfred became MP for Knaresborough between 1868 and 1874 and then for Bradford from 1880 to 1885, along with W.E. Forster.

Waller and Son

Spinning was not the only large-scale industry in Victorian Bradford, by any means. Waller's brewery of Trafalgar Street typifies that diversification which always happened in the northern towns as they grew in economic security and spread their wings to other sources of profit. Waller had a wine and spirit business in the city, based in Ivegate and Millergate, but the brewery was the centre, founded in 1847 by Charles Waller.

By the end of the century, T.W. Waller was producing light ales, bitter, stout and porter. The science and craft of the brewer's trade was celebrated with reference to Waller's in the grand-sounding pages of the Anti-Adulteration Review, which said: 'In Bradford the beers of Messrs Waller and son are spoken of by our analyst as possessing not only the proper gravity, alcoholic strength and freedom from acidity, but also having a flavour most pleasing to the palate, and a brilliant sparkling appearance to please the eye of the consumer...'

There was also wine to be considered. Waller's were game to try anything in their trade, and they stocked everything from port to champagne. They owned several public houses and hotels around Bradford, including the Royal Hotel in Low Moor, the Holme Lane Hotel, Dudley Hill, and the Fox and Hounds at Shipley.

Along with most of their counterpart northern tycoons, Waller's stepped in to do public good works and philanthropy, notably on one occasion when it was discovered that some Bradford emigrants to Brazil had fallen on hard times; the brewers gave the huge sum of £500 to bring the people back home. It can be imagined just how much that increased Waller's' local reputation.

Smaller but Fine: Fortune and Bentham

The engineers sprang up of course, as the demand for their expertise increased, and in the worsted industry it was natural that there would be a demand for the local production of combing machines. Fortune and Bentham of Richmond Road were typical of that lateral expansion in commerce as demand and supply accelerated.

The two engineers formed their partnership in 1879 and they present us with a perfect example of that process whereby the skills of the artisan in that period provided a base from which growth could be achieved. They stepped into the local commercial world and promoted their skills, first in a small way and then expanding.

They won contracts and made the right kind of connections. Their products were made to match very specific needs in the industry, or, as the point was made in the language of 1890, their work is, 'very largely supplemented by ingenious devices peculiar to the establishment; amongst which special mention must be made of an automatic contrivance for the making and drilling of fallers and circles for wool-combing machines.'

As well as inventing things to solve problems in the process of other firms, Fortune and Bentham did have a speciality. They made circles for a system called the Ratus, 'for the production of which they have achieved world-wide renown', one commentator has written. For this they won the gold medal at the Royal Yorkshire Jubilee Exhibition in Saltaire. Everything about this company indicates what the template was for success from small beginnings to a very important status and respect within the business community. The evolution of artisan into businessman was ever more frequent in the Victorian years.

The Cravenette Company

One example of many clothing specialists who sprang up as secondary industries in the clothing trade is the Cravenette company of Booth Street. They specialised in waterproof clothing. Mr T.F. Wiley came up with a fabric that was 'impervious to rain...but porous', and soon the Cravenette logo and name were leading the field in that special manufacture.

Wiley approached the American market and did very well, and the advantages of the new cloth were soon widely appreciated, the secret of that success being explained by a writer in *The Economist* periodical: 'The great advantage about the Cravenette process is that, while it makes the cloth so that rain runs off the surface, a free ventilation is left which makes it healthier than the old rubber goods which do not permit of free ventilation.'

Cravenette advertisement.

Apparently, 'eminent physicians' had stated that it was better to 'go wet than to be coated with rubber'. The public relations people at the firm were anxious to tell local writers that they were protecting their patent energetically, and that 'Like all goods of merit, Cravenette has its imitations which are unsatisfactory. Wideawake buyers will see to it that every garment bears the stamp.'

Naturally, the worsted industry dominated the town in this period. By about 1810 there were five mills and a population of 16,000; by 1831 there were 30 mills and 43,527 people, and by 1890 there were almost 240,000 people, a very large proportion of these employed in worsted manufacture. But we should not forget the smaller businesses, as they indicate not only the signs of change and new directions, but also testify to the health of the major concerns. Not only did Bradford have an abundance of dyers and finishers, but it was not difficult to find makers of 'fancy dress stuff' or even hearth-rugs around the city in 1890. James Burnley (see Chapter 16) had a love of celebrating in print 'Gigantic Businesses', but he also understood the nature of the small beginnings that produced millionaires, as in the case of waste products: the classic example is Samuel Cunliffe-Lister, who saw the potential in waste in the silk industry. As Burnley wrote, after describing how Cunliffe-Lister saw the messy waste products:

> 'After examining the heap and making a few enquiries, he bargained for the refuse – not a difficult matter – which ultimately was deposited within the precincts of Manningham Mills.'

The snapper up 'of unconsidered trifles' became a millionaire, truly a rags to riches story in Bradford.

NINE

Joseph Wright: Dialect Expert

'The details of Joseph Wright's life read like a romance. But it is romance which is built on a solid foundation of character and indomitable will.'

W.J. Halliday

I have headed this chapter with the word 'expert' and that is true of this great scholar. But he was much more than that. His life is truly amazing, in that he came from a poor background and was self-taught, yet in 1888 his first book was published, and its title was *Comparative Grammar of the Indo-Germanic Languages*. He had spent some time in Heidelberg, having saved £40 from his mill work, and completed his doctorate on *Qualitative and Quantitative Changes of the Indo-Germanic Vowel System in Greek*. Yet Joseph Wright could easily have become just another learned scholar like so many others with narrow academic interests.

Joseph Wright, 1925.

He did far more than that and, Yorkshire matters aside, all students of language and tradition owe to him the existence of the magnificent *English Dialect Dictionary*, six volumes of linguistic treasures, all opening up the past social history of England in a novel and fascinating way. He also set in motion a long tradition of dialect study in Yorkshire, later to flower in the University of Leeds School of English and elsewhere.

Poor Beginnings

Joseph Wright was born in Thackley, Idle, in 1855. As his family were so poor, there was a period when they all lived in the workhouse at Clayton, but his mother's hard work and dedication more than made up for the problems created by his feckless father, and Joseph also absorbed the work ethic, starting work at six and driving a donkey cart for 10 hours a day. By the age of seven he was doing mill work, first as a doffer at Salts Mill. When he was in his early teens he became a wool-sorter and then had some part-time schooling; he taught himself to read, using the periodical *Cassells' Popular Educator* and, of course, the Bible. His main affection in the world of learning was in the study of languages, and he taught himself the basics of Latin as well as French and German.

It was an age of autodidacts; working men had been grafting hard to get some kind of education during the decades of the growth of trade unions and mechanics' institutes. In Yorkshire learning was respected, and in a commercial age young men acquired practical learning as well as theoretical; Wright's first paper qualification was in shorthand.

His life was tough in the extreme, and in his wife's biography of him we have an account of his time in Saltaire: 'It is the duty of a doffer to remove the full bobbins from the spindle of the spinning-frame and replace them by empty ones. There are 144 spindles on one frame, 72 on each side. As a half-timer, Joseph Wright worked one week from 6 a.m. till 12.30 with half an hour's interval for breakfast, and the next week from 1.15 p.m. till 5.30 p.m.'

He must have been tired as he read his very difficult books, but the desire to learn was strong; the tale is told that it was the news from the Franco-Prussian War of 1870 that motivated him to read, and the amazing thing is that his mother, at the age of 45, also learned to read so that she could enter at least some of that world of literature her son was moving into.

Germany and Oxford

Wright went to Germany to increase his knowledge of the language and of course, to a scholar who was to specialise in the Germanic languages, it was essential. It was not easy, as he had to teach as well as learn. In Leipzig, for instance, he taught Old English and Philology. But there was some excitement, as it was not all book-learning with Wright, who liked to be heard and to be involved in life. He joked later in life that he would be arrested if ever he returned to Leipzig, as he explains: 'There was a strike of compositors going on and the result was a 'state of siege' enforced by the government. I was arrested in the Ton Halle for making a speech in sympathy with the strikers. I was a firebrand in those days...'

He was so determined that if we put together his quick intellect with the capacity for long hours of concentrated work, we can understand his words when explaining himself to his wife, saying, 'I am accustomed to get the very thing I want. When I once make up my mind that such a thing is the right thing to take place, I move almost heaven and earth to see that it *shall* take place.'

In Germany he wrote books and also did translations to keep the money flowing in; he even wrote a primer of Middle High German and that was published and ran to several editions. But he was bound for home and Oxford, returning in 1888. There he gave lectures and worked on his books, but as far as Yorkshire is concerned it was his interest in dialects that made his connection to Bradford so interesting, as he did much to preserve the language that so many amateur writers and historians had been writing or collecting for some time.

He made many friends in Oxford, and he worked hard in all kinds of extra duties, including marking examination papers, but in 1890 he was appointed to a lectureship in Teutonic Philology, a post created especially for him, so he had a proper foothold at last in the academic community. By 1892 he was deputy professor of Comparative Philology.

The English Dialect Dictionary

Wright said that it was this dictionary by which he wanted to be remembered. He had always had an interest in English dialects and in 1893 he wrote his *Windhill Dialect Grammar.* There had been an English Dialect Society in existence since the 1870s, and the Yorkshire Dialect

Society was formed in 1897, an organisation that was formed after a request from Wright for Yorkshire contributions. W.J. Halliday explains what happened: 'Contributions, consisting in all of about 35,000 words and phrases from some 90 persons, were sent to the editor on the eve of the dissolution of the committee in February 1897, it was decided to carry on the work of dialect research...'

Compiling a dictionary is a massive task of course. Such an undertaking requires substantial financial backing and a great deal of organisation. At the time, the great scholar W.W. Skeat was the leading light in the English Dialect Society and he had prompted the project, settling on Wright as the ideal man to edit the work. At the inception of the work there was simply a mass of paper material: there were a million slips of paper, weighing almost a ton. In a pre-computer age, the approach was to write definitions and usages of vocabulary on slips of paper and then sift them and catalogue them. But there had been haphazard collecting and little sense of organisation. The editor of such a massive work also needs a huge personal library so that linguistic descriptions and cross-references may be made.

The financial aspect was the most problematical. In the end, the method of publication chosen was by subscription. This was a tried and tested method in publications with a circumscribed readership and it was worthwhile, but of course hundreds of people had to be approached – and by letter. Subscribers had to be shown the value of the task, and so a prospectus was also issued. In a period of five months, Wright wrote 3,000 letters.

There was progress as the task continued, however. Wright was given a Civil List pension of £200 a year and he and his staff of three were given the use of an office. To this base came information from a group of correspondents across the country – a thousand people altogether.

The momentous date came: 1 July 1896, the date of the publication of the first part of the dictionary; following that the whole work was gradually assembled, being made up of six volumes in total. Not only does the dictionary give a definition and etymology, but there are also extensive lists of variants, so that the Yorkshire word 'addle' for instance, meaning 'to earn or work for', is given in forms similar to that found in other counties.

Wright's workshop.

Bradford, being the home of so many popular and successful local dialect poets, storytellers and comedians, welcomed the work Wright gave to the literary and historical communities. It was an achievement that would appeal to both scholars of the English language and to general readers with an interest in the words and speech of specific places.

Elizabeth Mary Lea, Mrs Wright

Wright married one of his students at Oxford, Elizabeth. She was to become not only his wife, but also co-author with him. They married in 1896 and then she worked with Joseph on *Old and Middle English Grammars*, and wrote a book of her own, *Rustic Speech and Folklore*, published in 1913. Elizabeth wrote her husband's biography in 1934, *Joseph Wright, Man and Scholar*, and in that she makes extensive use of his letters and writings, and gives a great deal of information about how and why this extraordinary man achieved so much. But she also recounts their life together.

He was a serious and demanding teacher. Elizabeth quotes a letter he sent to her in which he wrote: 'Perseverance and patience form great factors in study. After pointing out to you in this way once for all how

A page from the *Dialect Dictionary*.

important it is to be *very accurate*, I feel sure that your written work will be quite satisfactory in the future.'

They had a remarkable and happy life on the whole. Wright wrote at one point that it was always such a comfort to him to feel that they had trust in each other and that they could 'pour out their hearts' when needed. They settled in Oxford and he had a house made, called 'Thackley', and made sure it had a Yorkshire roof, among other things. Wright was a devoted family man and a doting husband. The photographs of him show his fatherliness – a quality that his students pointed out in him as well.

ADDLE

ADDLE, *v.* In all the northern counties to n.Ches., Notts., Staff., Leic., Linc., Nhamp., Rut., e.Anglia; not in Sc. Not in gloss. of s.Ches. and Shr. Also written **adle** N.Cy. RAY, Linc. SKINNER; **aadle** Suff. MOOR; **eddle** N.Cy. BROCKETT, Nhumb. HESLOP, Cumb. GIBSON, Yks. WILLAN; **yeddle** n.Ches. WILBRAHAM; **aidle** Nhumb. HESLOP, Linc. BROGDEN, e.Anglia, FORBY; **aydle** c. and **ettle** n.Cumb. DICKINSON.
Pron. adl—Besides adl there occur also edl in Nhumb., Cumb., ēdl in Nhumb., c.Cumb., Linc., e.Anglia; ettle n.Cumb., and yedl in n.Ches.
1. To earn, acquire by one's labour.
N.Cy. RAY *Collection of N.Cy. Words* (1691); HUTTON *Tour to the Caves* (1781); BROCKETT *Gloss.* (1846). **Nhumb.** He addles three ha'pence a week, That's nobbut a fardin' a day (Song, 'Ma Laddie'), HESLOP *Gloss.* (1892). **Dur.** *Teesdale Gloss.* (1849). **Cumb.** I's gān to eddle me five shillin' middlin' cannily, GIBSON *Folk-speech of Cumb.* (1869) p. 2; FERGUSON *Gloss.* (1873); *c.* aydle, *s. w.* addle, *n.* ettle, DICKINSON *Gloss.* (1878). **s.Westm.** Ye dunnet addle as mickle ta day, HUTTON *Storth and Arnside Dialogues* (1760) l. 29. **Yks.** *n.* Sha's t'aud (too old) te addle better waage, MUNBY *Verses New and Old* (1865) p. 70; Ah's nowght bud what Ah addles, ATKINSON *Cleveland Gloss.* (1868); HARLAND *Swaledale Gloss.* (1873); F. K. ROBINSON *Whitby Gloss.* (1876); *e.* He cannot addle his bread, MARSHALL *Rural Economy* (1788) EDS. (1873); Ah haint addled saut (salt) ti my taty this mornin, ROSS, STEAD, HOLDERNESS *Holderness Gloss.* (1877); *n.* and *e.* He addles a good waage, MORRIS *Yks. Folk-Talk* (1892); *mid.* When he'd addled his shun (shoes), BLACKAH *Songs and Poems* (1867) p. 13 [said of a horse when it falls upon its back and rolls from one side to the other. When a horse does this in Hants. and Suss., it is said to earn a gallon of oats, HOLLOWAY *Gloss.* (1839)]; C. C. ROBINSON *Gloss.* (1876); *w.* We mun teugh an addle summat, CARR *Craven Dial.* (1828) ii. p. 289; It isn't what a chap addles, it's what a chap saves 'at makes him rich, HARTLEY *Yks. Budget* (1868) p. 48; eddle (pron. addle), WILLAN *Archaeologia* (1811) vol. xvii. p. 145; HUNTER *Hallamshire Gloss.* (1829); BANKS *Wakefield Gloss.* (1865); EASTHER *Huddersfield Gloss.* (1883); ADDY *Sheffield Gloss.* (1888). **Lanc.** He addled about eight shillin' a week, WAUGH *Home Life Lanc. Factory Folk* (1867) p. 10a; NODAL and MILNER *Gloss.* (1875); He says he's addled fifty pund, HARLAND *Lyrics* (1866) p. 76; I'm like the little donkeys i' the lane, I canna addle nought, *Stone edge* (1868) ch. x. p. 134; *n.* MORRIS *Furness Gloss.* (1869); *s.* COLLIER *Tim Bobbin* (edit. 1811) p. 62. **Ches.** WILBRAHAM *Gloss.* (1820); LEIGH *Gloss.* (1877); HOLLAND *Gloss.* (1886). **Derb.** PEGGE *Derbicisms* (†1796) EDS. (1894). **Notts.** MUSTERS *MSS. Gloss.* **Linc.** SKINNER *Etymologicon* (1671); I have aidled my week's wages, BROGDEN *Gloss.* (1866); Mun be a guvness, lad, or summut, and addle her bread, TENNYSON *Northern Farmer*, New Style (1870) st. 7; *n.* Tom Stocks can addle fower shillin' a daay at suffin', PEACOCK *Gloss.* (1889); *s.w.* COLE *Gloss.* (1886). **Staff.** POOLE *Gloss.* (1880). **Leic.** Oi ha' addled my weej, EVANS *Gloss.* (1881). **Nhamp.** STERNBERG *Dial. and Folklore* (1851); BAKER *Gloss.* (1854). **Rut.** WORDSWORTH *Gloss.* (1891). **e.Anglia.** FORBY *Gloss.* (1830).

ORIGINAL SPECIMEN OF THE E.D.D.
which proved much too long

He was a man who loved a good story and liked to entertain. One of his favourite tales was of a trip on a train near Bradford when Leeds had been playing Bradford at football and Bradford had won. He heard a man say, 'Ah tell ye what 'tis, ye Leeds loiners are goin' dahn so much in t' world, at ye'll ev tae v letters addressed to Leeds, near Bradford suin.'

Joseph Wright died in 1930, a man who can safely lay claim to being one of Bradford's true originals, a uniquely gifted man who rose above his social conditions and taught himself not only to be a great scholar, but also a gentleman and a good friend. He will be remembered as the father of dialect study and as an exemplary Yorkshireman, warm, direct and constant, with a relish of hard graft and of working with others to achieve wonderful things. He is buried in Wolvercote cemetery, Oxford, far away from Worstedopolis, but he is certainly not forgotten there.

TEN

Sir Titus Salt

'History is the essence of innumerable biographies'
Thomas Carlyle

There are perhaps three or four candidates in history who might lay claim to being 'Mr Bradford' and surely Titus Salt would be a leading contender. My quotation from Carlyle indicates that men make what we call history, but some men shape affairs more than others. We use the phrase 'mover and shaker' today of an entrepreneur; it could have been coined to define Titus Salt. The model industrial community of his Saltaire on the River Aire was one of many such forward-looking places and was not the first, as we look back to New Lanark and Robert Owen, but it may well be the most impressive.

The course of Salt's life shows most of the established clichés of the rise of the industrial magnate of his age: he was born into a Non-conformist family in Morley in 1803 and pictures of his family home, the Old Manor House, hint at nothing special. But he then learned the skills required in the wool trade and used those skills to combine with an exceptionally acute business brain and thought on a broad canvas, expanding his mills as he progressed. After that came civic honours and then national honours.

That scenario reads like a typical plot line in a regional saga or a biography of

Sir Titus S
By Laura (

any one of a thousand northern entrepreneurs who 'made it' in the tough world of the clothing industry. However, that outline says nothing about Salt's very special qualities and his stunningly grand achievements.

A Summary of his Rise

In 1822, the Salt family moved to Bradford where Titus's father, Daniel, opened a wool stapling concern. At the same time Titus was learning the range of skills involved: sorting, weaving and all the rest in that local industry. Titus was apprenticed to the firm of William Rouse and Sons on the Bradford Canal when he reached 19 and later joined his father's company in 1824. He was only 33 when he was striking out on his own, and his knack of taking educated risks for creative innovation paid off after he bought alpaca wool in order to make a more refined fabric.

In 1830 he married Caroline Whitlam, daughter of a sheep farmer in north Lincolnshire, and the couple were married in Grimsby parish church.

He then bought some land at Saltaire, mainly because of the negative social and environmental forces at work in Bradford itself. The 1840s had seen terrible working conditions in the town, along with a dangerous level of pollution which affected public health and brought about a high mortality rate. Times were hard, especially for the woolcombers, who had begun to look after their own affairs by forming a Woolcombers Protective association. There was no doubt that such horrors as cholera and typhus were at work in the town, and next to that there was the noxious atmosphere around Bradford beck, known as 'River Stink' in the area.

More than that, Titus wanted to create a community in which the degradation of the urban working classes, ruined by drink and moral decay, would be avoided and new possibilities opened up for social good.

Saltaire took a long time to create, but was finally finished by 1868, when he was 65. In that same year he opened New Mill by the canal – a place with both a spinning house and a dye works. Typical of Salt was the way he worked out a method of using the waste water on the site via a turbine. New Mill chimney was based on the campanile of the Church of Santa Maria Gloriosa in Venice.

He then made time to be involved in politics, leaving his sons (particularly Titus junior) to take care of the business. He had always

Grimsby parish church, where Salt was married.

been active in that sphere, but in the years 1859-1861 he was MP for Bradford, as a Liberal. Young Titus ran the family firm, after marrying the daughter of another wealthy local businessman, Francis Crossley of Halifax.

In 1869 Titus was nationally recognised and rewarded for his achievement by being given a knighthood. He became Sir Titus Salt of Saltaire. But the honours did not end there: Napoleon III created him a Knight of the Legion of Honour and other honours followed. In terms of Bradford, the most visible honour was the erection of his statue in Town Hall Square in 1871.

Sir Titus Salt died on 29 December 1876. His son Titus followed the business path of his famous father, but he died in 1887, aged only 44, and by 1892 the company was no more, having been liquidated.

Saltaire

A writer in 1950 called Saltaire 'a solid, ugly town with its huge mill overshadowing all'. Salt had grasped that the wool of the donskoi, the long-haired Russian sheep, was suitable for worsted. The result was alpaca, and from that emerged the empire of which Saltaire was the pride and joy. A Mr Fairbairn, interviewed by Lettice Cooper 50 years ago, was the man who made the mill steam engines, and he said that Saltaire made in one year 'enough alpaca cloth to reach over land and sea to Peru, the native mountains of the alpaca'.

Salt staged an opening banquet when Saltaire was complete; this was in the mill counting-house and the menu was based on a supply of 40 chines of beef, 120 legs of mutton, 100 lamb platters, 40 hams and 50 pigeon pies. But it was not all simply a case of public 'spin'. Salt was genuinely interested in the moral welfare of his employees. He was a devout Christian, a Congregationalist and Liberal, who saw the ills of the side-effects of the Industrial Revolution and believed that a man of power should also be a man of responsibility. In practical terms, he was convinced that a family home was the right basis for a morally upright life and for respectable values; he built a school, guarded by two stone lions which symbolised Determination and Vigilance. He also paid attention to the homes, making back gardens and adding indoor fittings and more bedrooms than the norm.

Opinions may differ on the attraction of the massive Congregational church at Saltaire (Cooper thought it 'hideous'), but it is unmistakably there, a massive presence. The kind of reasoning behind all this was explained in contemporary terms in a magazine called *The British Workman* and *Home Monthly*, which, in a profile of Titus Salt, wrote this: 'Money brings no inward delight to the finest faculties. Honour cries, Come up to me! But he who attains the prize of distinction, is weary of the hard climb...The preacher next morning met one of his hearers. It was the well-known millionaire...Sir Titus Salt...'

The magazine made Salt's determination to be 'weary' in spite of his wealth into a moral lecture, with the conclusion that 'The employer who treats those under him with discourtesy is generally coming to be considered a second-rate businessman...Courtesy is a characteristic of the strong and able; in business, as in social relations, kindliness marks those who are of the first grade.'

Titus Salt had attained the level of benevolent celebrity, and that in an age of philanthropy and commerce often living uneasily together. But the fact is there under all that myth and public interest: he had 4,000 employees at Saltaire at its height in around 1880. It is an incredible thought to envisage Titus looking at all those local people and to reflect on how they were part of a social experiment, and one that showed both creativity and flair in its design.

The Salt Homes

One of the most fascinating aspects of the Titus Salt story is the nature, design and sheer impact of the homes built by the Salts. Arguably the most impressive is Crow Nest at Lightcliffe, where Titus Salt lived between the years of 1844 and 1858. Most of the substance of the building was designed by John Carr of Horbury, Wakefield, perhaps most famous for his work at York Castle prison and on the York Fairfax House. He also designed Pye Nest near Halifax.

Methley Hall, near Castleford, had always been the home of the Earls of Mexborough, and the older Elizabethan foundation and shell had been developed in the middle of the 18th century. By 1830 the current earl joined the enthusiasm for Gothic Revival and Methley Hall was transformed again. Titus was there from 1858 to 1867.

There are many perspectives from which we may see and judge this truly remarkable man. He was entrepreneur, inventor, true original in a bustling and creative period of industrial history, philanthropist and perhaps, above all, a massive paternal figure who seemed in his time to define that spirit of Bradford: independence yet also brotherhood, and individual initiative, but also good teamwork in business. He contributed to so many good causes that it is hard to single out any for special mention, but in Bradford he founded scholarships for Bradford Grammar School, and further afield he contributed to the costs of building the Albert Hall. His social good work and caring attitude regarding his own area was evident in the massive event of his funeral in 1876; over 100,000 people were there on the route of the cortège as it crawled along to his final resting place, the Salt mausoleum.

Salt's Mill is now a World Heritage Centre, defined as such by UNESCO. Titus conceived his mill and community as an experiment in living in terms of a concord between work and home life. Saltaire is many things to many people, but to a majority of right-minded Victorians, it would have given a physical form to that dream of a community adhering to the gospel of Christian life and commitment with the credo of 'labor omnia vincit' (work overcomes all – the motto of Bradford).

ELEVEN

Did Jack the Ripper Come to Town?

'Dear Boss, I keep on hearing that the police have caught me,
but they can't fix me yet…'

Very probably the words of Jack himself

In the 'Ripper year' of 1888, there was a flood of hoax letters to the police. Clearly, such hoaxes are a very stupid and dangerous activity. The culprits are very difficult to track down, but Bradford appears to be the only place in which a writer of such a letter was caught and charged. She was Maria Coroner, a Canadian-born milliner living in Westgrove Street, a woman with a dark side. She had written to the local newspaper and to the chief constable, saying when caught that she had done it as a joke, and the whole affair attracted a large media interest when she appeared in court on 23 October that year.

Maria was fined £20 and bound over to keep the peace for six months. One newspaper report said that 'a dense crowd fought for admission to the court'. It has disturbing echoes of Wearside Jack and the Yorkshire Ripper hoax in our own time. But in an age when the popular press made great sensational tales out of commonplace domestic killings, the strange twisted fantasy that produced 'Ripper letters' can to a certain extent be understood.

The Maria Coroner case was a curiosity, but we can add to that something far more startling and intriguing that happened in Bradford that year – it may have been the Ripper himself who came north to kill, perhaps after taunting the Metropolitan Police with his own terrible letters.

'The Discovery of Jack the Ripper's First Murder' (Famous Crimes journals, 1900)

The Body Found

Just after Christmas 1888, John Gill of Thorncliff Road went for a ride on a milk cart. It was very early in the morning, and his mother never saw him alive again. He had been seen playing but also, menacingly, he was seen talking to a man, a stranger to the area by all accounts. The family soon felt the distress of his absence and feared the worst; they placed a poster on view, with a physical description of him, and actually used the word 'lost' despite the fact that it was only a day after his disappearance.

John, eight years old, was found in a stable by Joe Buckle, a butcher. Joe was cleaning the place when he came across an indescribable object. On looking closer he saw that it was a corpse, and most noticeable on first inspection was the fact that one ear had been sliced off. He ran for help. Later, when a closer inspection was made by officers, it was found that there had been extreme mutilation of the body; John's stomach had been cut open and vital organs placed on top of him. He had been repeatedly cut and stabbed in the chest, and there was a rough noose around his neck.

This is where the complex business of the massive number of Ripper letters figures in the story. The pathology certainly makes the Gill murder a contender for being classified as a Ripper killing; Dr Bond in London, when writing about the body of victim Mary Kelly, noted that 'the viscera were found in various parts...the liver between the feet and the spleen by the left side of the body'. There are similarities, but the main argument for the Ripper coming north rests on the statements made in the letters. As Philip Sugden has written, 'The important question is...whether any of these letters we have noticed was written by the murderer.' This was said about the first letter received, well before the Bradford case. By the time of the Gill killing, police were walking into Whitechapel in pairs and detectives were everywhere around the area. Five killings had taken place in London, the last in November, just a month before the Bradford case.

A Scrap of Newspaper

At the end of November, one of the Ripper letters contained the words, 'I shall do another murder on some young youth such as printing lads who work in the city. I did write you once before...I shall do them worse than the women, I shall take their hearts...' The crime writer, Patricia

Cornwell, believes that the Bradford murder is worth serious consideration. But the problem with Patricia Cornwell's use of the Ripper letters in associating the Bradford case with Jack is that she talks of the 'Ripper letter' as if their provenance is certified and that certain examples cluster together as the work of individual authors (see her book, *Portrait of a Killer*). This is why she dismisses the most tantalising scrap of detail in poor John Gill's murder: that a piece of a Liverpool newspaper was used to wrap part of the body. Even more fascinating, the paper had a name on it: 'W. Mason, Derby Road.'

Those Ripperologists who think that the mystery killer was James Maybrick, merchant of Liverpool, would perhaps point to the fact that Maybrick was most probably meeting someone in Manchester at one point in 1888, but otherwise apparently never went near Bradford. Recent writing on Maybrick, and notably the new work done by handwriting and paper experts on the celebrated book *The Diaries of Jack the Ripper* would seem to confirm that there is no factual evidence for the Bradford connection. We have known for a long time that there was a Lancashire connection because of James Bierley from Rochdale, who was linked to the Maybrick family.

Walter Sickert

The Ripper letters in the hand of the painter Walter Sickert, whom Cornwell believes to have been the Ripper, also contain one text that reads, 'I riped [sic] up a little boy in Bradford.' The great Sherlock Holmes would have reacted to this by insisting that, though these Bradford letters may have been by the same hand, there is nothing to prove that they belonged to the man we know as Jack the Ripper. In other words, what we most likely have here is that well-known phenomenon in homicide, the copycat crime.

Bradford was, as Patricia Cornwell points out, a city on the tour being made by the great actor, Sir Henry Irving, and Sickert had been an actor and was fond of play-going. If he had gone north to distract affairs from Whitechapel, as Cornwell points out, 'Many of the cities mentioned in the Ripper letters were on Henry Irving's theatre company's schedule, which was published in the newspapers daily...' The same is said in her book about racecourses, another passion of Sickert's, and of course, it is not difficult to find racecourses near Bradford in 1888. This is all speculation, but interesting nevertheless.

The existence of the Bradford references open up new possibilities, but beneath all the hype and speculation we have the existence of such copycat crimes and the psychology of serial killing now very much established in academic study. The thought behind killer profiling does not find satisfactory lines of thought in the Gill murder. It is not convincing that the sexual-sadistic Ripper would switch to murders of young men, and also the use of the noose is bizarre as a scene of crime ritual communication, as such killers tend to do. Another curious detail on Gill's body was a piece of torn shirting about his neck – again, hardly a signature of the Ripper in London.

Conclusions

As far as the Bradford connection is concerned, the events could have turned out tragically for the prime local suspect, one Bill Barrett, a dairyman, but he was cleared after having 'a long interview' with his legal adviser that was undoubtedly the basis of a sound defence. The only evidence was circumstantial. If the killing was a copycat murder then the identity of the real killer remains a mystery, and the Gill case is in the annals of unsolved crimes.

The Bradford case is not the only one that may be another Ripper victim outside Whitechapel. In June 1887, at Temple Stairs on the Thames, parts of a body previously found at Rainham were found in a parcel. At the inquest it was asserted that someone with a knowledge of anatomy had done this ghastly murder. Eventually, as in this Bradford scenario, a letter supposedly from the 'real' Ripper denied any involvement with these body parts. At least the Bradford killing had some definite pointers to the actual Ripper.

TWELVE

From Haworth to the World

'Thus, children leading a secluded life are often thoughtful and dreamy'

Elizabeth Gaskell

It is not at all surprising that the Brontë family of Haworth should have had such a huge impact on the literary world, and on literary studies everywhere across the globe. Here we have a talented and highly creative family, three of whom became successful novelists, existing in the wilds of the moors, their creative spirits nurtured by the environment and by their rather impoverished lives in a village which was on the periphery of the Bradford literary scene. Yet Charlotte and Emily Brontë in particular made such an impact on the readership and publishing world of London that they became best-sellers in their day, and then classics afterwards, as critics and other writers realised their true achievements.

People write now of 'The Brontë Industry' and books have been written on the mediation of the 'myth' of the Brontë sisters, given to us in film, on radio, television, comic strips, graphic novels and in every other available medium. The novels *Jane Eyre* and *Wuthering Heights* are entrenched in the canon of English literature and it is hard to find a course or a textbook on the 19th-century writers which does not include the Brontë texts.

This remarkable story, beginning with the life of the father, Patrick Brontë, a poor scholar from County Down who made it to Cambridge, has become that 'fairytale' narrative which proves that ordinary people may aspire to be celebrity writers, even when their childhood circumstances are largely against such success. But the Victorian cultural machine soon absorbed these writers as celebrities and Haworth became a place to visit, a literary shrine. The early deaths of the writing sisters contributed to this, along with the astonishingly successful novels, and Mrs Elizabeth Gaskell's biography of Charlotte Brontë, which was published in 1857.

Patrick, the Father

The Revd Patrick Brontë was born in Ahaderg, Co. Down, on 17 March 1777. His original name, Prunty, was changed as part of his transformation when he grew older and won a scholarship as a sizar to St John's College, Cambridge, in 1802. It may well have been partly due to the Duke of Wellington's great popularity, as one of his titles was the Duke of Brontë. Patrick was a diligent student and rose from student to teacher by taking a post at a village school at Drumgoland in the same county.

His first curacy was in Essex and after that he moved to Yorkshire, first to Hartshead in 1811. Patrick had the urge to write, and his main publications were poems, often featuring rural Ireland and traditional poetic themes. His first collection was *Cottage Poems*, printed in Halifax. The general opinion of his poetry in his time was summed up by one commentator: they were 'not of a high order, yet evince considerable ability and genuine sentiment.'

The young parson made a friend of William Morgan, who had been appointed to serve at Bierley Chapel, Bradford, in the same year. As they both went to visit Mr Fennell, headmaster of the Wesleyan School at Apperley, they both also met young women who would be their future wives. An announcement in *The Gentleman's Magazine* explains what the development of these friendships was:

'Married, at Guiseley, near Bradford, by the Revd William Morgan, Minister of Bierley, Revd P. Brontë B.A., minister of Hartshead cum Clifton, to Maria, third daughter of the late T. Branwell Esq., of Penzance. And at the same time and place, by the Revd P. Brontë, Revd W. Morgan to the only daughter of Mr John Fennell, Head Master of the Wesleyan Academy, near Bradford.'

Patrick then moved to Thornton, where Charlotte, Emily and Anne were born. He had already had two daughters, Maria and Elizabeth, while at Hartshead. Then the family moved to more spacious housing in

Haworth when Patrick was given the living there, along with a larger income. But tragedy was running in the seam of the family structure: Maria Brontë suffered from cancer and died, after a terrible period of suffering, in 1821 after the elder two daughters had both died while away at school at Cowan Bridge, near Kirby Lonsdale.

The picture we have of Patrick Brontë in that formative period for the writers at Haworth parsonage owes a lot to Mrs Gaskell; he is given to the world as an eccentric who loved to fire his pistols into the back garden and to be so negligent a parent that he left his children to make their own entertainment until they were old enough to work as governesses or tutors. He was far more than this, and was destined to outlive all his children. Regarding his one son, Patrick, the relationship was complex. Young Patrick, the darling of his father's eye, was meant to be a scholar and was given the opportunity of the best schooling his father could afford; as he grew older he became a dilettante, restless and troubled in his mind. His father supported him in every failing venture, and what remained at the heart of the young man was an unrealistic self-belief that regularly cast him into depression.

Branwell

Patrick Branwell Brontë (his full name) was known as Branwell generally, and he certainly had talent as an artist, as his work at Haworth Parsonage Museum shows. He fancied himself as a poet, and he had the temerity to write to William Wordsworth asking for a critique of his work. He knew how to flatter and present himself shamelessly, as in these words: 'Do pardon me, sir, that I have ventured to come before one whose works I have most loved in our literature, and who most has been with me a divinity of the mind – laying before him one of my writings, and asking of him a judgement of its contents…My aim, sir, is to push out into the open world, and for this I trust not poetry alone…'

Branwell declined into addiction to both alcohol and laudanum and, although he worked at times, even on the railway at Hebden Bridge, generally his sad life contains failures, false starts, loss of self-confidence, mistaken friendships and pathetic arguments. It may be that he was destined to be the kind of man who is very popular at the local (the Black Bull at Haworth) as he was a live wire full of stories and wisecracks, but

Haworth Parsonage.

inside he was an empty shell, a superficial character with a need for affection and display.

But what cannot be denied is that he played a part in the imaginative development of his three famous sisters. When the children first invented imaginary lands, as children often do, they made the places of Gondal and Angria, and paired up. Emily and Anne made Gondal and Charlotte and Branwell made Angria. These stories, with combinations of words and colourful drawings, were done meticulously and with a sense of commitment to a fantasy, while at the same time the invented places were linked to the real world of the time in references and veiled events. These are seen now as part of the groundwork of the future novelists, in

Haworth Church.

The parsonage doorway, Haworth.

The Black Bull, Branwell's favourite hostelry.
By Laura Carter.

terms of how a 'world' is made through people, events and descriptions. Branwell was a part of that, and we can imagine his envy when the sisters progressed as writers and he did not.

Charlotte

Charlotte and Emily were sent to the school at Cowan Bridge, but then went on to Roe Head under the tutelage of Miss Wooler; they had also had tuition at home and in the local school. Cowan Bridge, where their older sisters had died of TB, was clearly a high-risk affair and the girls were withdrawn. The experience did provide some of the material for Charlotte's *Jane Eyre*, however: nothing was to be wasted as 'material' for Charlotte the novelist. She also went to work as a teacher in Belgium, and there she gathered the material for the substance of what was to be her first completed (but last published) novel, *The Professor*.

It was Charlotte who undertook the task of getting the sisters into print, as the long periods spent around the big table at Haworth, writing and drawing, began to produce stories and poems in profusion. She negotiated for a self-publishing venture which eventually became the Brontës' first published work: *Poems by Currer, Ellis and Acton Bell*. In that way the three *noms de plume* were created which would be soon on the spines of their respective published novels: Currer was Charlotte, Emily was Ellis and Anne Acton. They had all certainly been busy. One Victorian biographer summarised the early situation in this way: 'This brings us to the literary activity of the trio of sisters. Already in their earliest years, as soon as the use of pen and paper became familiar, they essayed themselves in literary compositions and we are told that they filled no less than 22 MS volumes with tales, essays, poems, plays etc. When it is remembered, too, that the mental pabulum provided for his family by the Revd P. Brontë comprised *The British Essayist*, *The Rambler*, *The Mirror*, we need feel little surprise at the tersely classical style of writing to which the sisters attained...'

Top Withins.

The writer pointed out the basis of their literary style, and quite rightly indicated the fact that their successes were all the more amazing because of that. They had to have a contemporary feel as well. This they gained from reading the more current journals and newspapers available at the library of the Keighley Mechanics' Institute, a few miles away.

Charlotte's massive success with her novel *Jane Eyre* is well known. The firm of Smith, Elder published this work, which was an immediate sensation, dealing not only with issues of women's place in society, but with the nature of love and friendship, religious faith and with that Victorian dilemma, the interplay between duty and the individual life. She published *Villette* and *Shirley* before *The Professor*, and made a number of famous literary friends and correspondents. Charlotte was the hit of more than one season for the London literati and all indications are that she enjoyed that immensely.

She married Arthur Bell Nicholls, a curate at Haworth, in June 1854. By that time both her sisters were dead and she was nurse to her ageing father. But less than a year after the marriage Charlotte herself died, in March 1855. Her father lived on to be 84, dying at Haworth in June 1861.

Anne Brontë's grave in Scarborough, St Mary's Church.

St Mary's Church.

Emily

Despite the fact that Emily Brontë could apply herself to structured, ordered work, such as learning German from a grammar while baking in the Haworth kitchens, the image she has in the mythology of English literature is that of a wild, free soul, roaming the moors in spirit, a child of Romanticism. All that is from her words in her only novel, of course, but we lose track of the 'rational being' Mrs Gaskell referred to. Arguably, the legends about her also come partly from her highly unusual personal qualities – her tough stoicism and her element of aggressive, violent action, as in her handling of her fierce dog, Keeper.

Emily lived just 30 years, dying in 1848 on 19 December. In her lifetime *Wuthering Heights* was not really understood and appreciated. Margaret Drabble writes that her main difference from Charlotte was her isolation and self-sufficiency: 'Unlike Charlotte, she had few close friends, wrote few letters and had but few strong loyalties.'

As well as being placed high in the rank of novelists, Emily has been recognised as a truly individual and talented poet. Of the three sisters, her nature as a poet is generally seen to be the best, and her sources, from reading, dreaming and personal vision, strengthen her poetry, giving more to it than the average expression of middle of the road Victorian beliefs which are so common in the verse of the time.

One of the mysteries of the Brontë story is that there may have been a second novel from Emily in progress. A letter with the date of February 1848 was once found in her writing desk, and this was from her publishers (addressed to Ellis Bell) with a hint that there was a second novel in gestation. The publisher, Newby, definitely wanted a second book. But after Emily's death, Charlotte destroyed her sister's personal effects, and many have speculated as to why this was. What we do know, from Charlotte's preface to Emily's novel in a later edition, is that she disapproved of Emily's excess of emotive language and themes of destructive love – the Romanticism she had in her that may make Charlotte's version of those beliefs quite tame and civilised.

Anne

Anne has repeatedly been labelled the sister who was quiet and gentle. Indeed she was, but her novel *The Tenant of Wildfell Hall* (1848), an attempt to particularise her themes of gender relationships so central to her thought, suggests from the title a work similar to Emily's. Anne was often in steady work as a tutor and governess, the latter being a central character in her first novel, *Agnes Grey*, a work which made her contemporaries give a second thought to those underpaid and exploited workers in the homes of the rich and prosperous new middle classes.

She died at Scarborough on 28 May 1849, aged only 29, and she is buried in St Mary's churchyard below the castle. Anne was another victim of tuberculosis and she suffered horribly, trying all kinds of medicines, including some quack remedies. When she died the old servant at Haworth, Tabitha, never forgave Charlotte for allowing the youngest sister to be buried away from home.

THIRTEEN

A Catalogue of Criminals

'The case excited much interest, it being known that the Culprit was a clergyman.'

Dickens's *Household Narrative*

Bradford has seen its share of brutal crimes, and has experienced all versions of horrific murder, from the Victorian garrotters to the Yorkshire Ripper, but there are thousands of other crimes in the records, some insane, some absurd and some entertaining in their sheer stupidity. This is a selection of some of the more unusual ones from the 1800s.

Uttering by the Vicar

In the language of crime, uttering does not mean speaking: it refers to the crime of forgery, a very serious offence which until the 1820s in England was punishable by death. In 1853 one of the more bizarre examples of this criminality took place, and the culprit was a vicar, the Revd Beresford. He forged an endorsement of a bill for the sum of £100 – a great deal of money at the time. The case was sensational locally because he was a clergyman but also 'highly connected, and next heir to a peerage'.

In October 1849 Beresford called at the offices of the Bradford Banking Company and asked the manager to discount a bill from a London company called Hibbert. The practice then was for a bill like that to be signed and endorsed by a prominent person, so Beresford asked if such a signature from Mr Kay of Manningham Hall would be acceptable and was told it would be. What happened next was strange indeed.

A letter arrived at the bank, addressed to Beresford, and the clergyman arrived to collect it, opened it, and then presented it for discount. It had a signature purporting to be by Kay. The manager was suspicious as he was not convinced that the endorsement was genuine. There was the signature – John Cunliffe Kay. At that point, Beresford's conman skills came into play as he managed to persuade the manager that Kay had been ill when visited and would have had a shaky hand. The manager was impressed and discounted the bill.

Actually, Kay had been approached by Beresford but had refused to sign. Beresford then forged the signature, taking it from a letter written some time before. But fate was against the forger; he was not traced by any police work or by a smart detective. Kay accidentally met him walking in Regent Street and had him arrested. Kay, as a witness, recalled Beresford visiting the hall. What emerged was that some time before, the vicar had been introduced to Kay by his mother-in-law, as a relative of hers. It was noted in court that the accused 'Was a cousin of Lord Decies, and next heir to the peerage. He told Kay that he would be Lord Decies in the spring, that he was married and had a daughter of 15 years of age.

The counsel for the defence ran through half a dozen reasons why the prosecution was foolish and misguided, but Baron Martin, the judge, dismissed them all, insisting that the only points of interest were whether Beresford knowingly forged the signature and whether the endorsement was forged. The jury found Beresford guilty and he was sentenced to transportation for the period of his natural life. A report at the time was: 'On hearing the sentence, the prisoner seemed astounded; he staggered, and was removed from the dock supported by the officers. It was rumoured in court that he had a living in Cork of £1,000 a year, which has been sequestered for his debts.'

John Mann gets Six Months

At the court of appeal in 1914, John Mann and his counsel tried to overturn his sentence of six months imprisonment with hard labour. Mann's crime was against no one else, nor against any property. He had tried to take his own life and failed, and had therefore committed a crime – and that crime existed in England until 1961.

A satire on the struggle against street crime.

Mann and his lawyers tried to argue that a *felonia de se* (a crime against oneself) was not an actual felony. They wanted to have it defined as a lesser offence, a misdemeanour. What he did was a public attempt at suicide – or so it seemed. He was on a tram in Bradford, drunk, and suffering from the effects of taking some salts of lemon. That substance was a kind of mild bleach, so his sufferings in public were loud, disturbing and, for some, alarming in the extreme.

RATHER INCONSIDERATE

Policeman (suddenly, to street performer). " Now, then ! just you move on, will yer ? "

If his crime was a felony, then Mann could be given hard labour, and under the Hard Labour Act of 1823 that was reinforced. The defence lawyers tried another approach, saying that Mann had made a statement, not on oath, that he could not recall buying any salts of lemon and that it never entered his head in his life. But the appeal court found that such a matter would still not have changed the verdict.

Poor John Mann was clearly disturbed; he had tried to take his own life twice before that day on the Bradford tram. He needed therapy, not rock-breaking.

One of the Hangman's Worst Moments

This is a story of an argument that got well out of hand, and of the calamitous results of the confrontation – a tale of a fight in a public house, a quick death and a painful, agonising death. The man who ends the story is Thomas Askern, public hangman, a man subject to occasional terrible mistakes in his occupation.

It started on Boxing Day 1876, when 37-year-old John Johnson was enjoying a drink with Amelia Walker in the saloon of the Bedford Arms in Wakefield Road. Everything was convivial; they were enjoying each

ODD-HANDED JUSTICE.—*First Ruffian.* " Wot was I hup for, and wot 'ave I got ?
Well, I floor'd a woman and took 'er watch, and I've got two years and a floggin'."
Second Ruffian. " Ha !—*I* flung a woman out o' the top floor winder; an' I've on'y got
three months ! " *First Ruffian.* " Ah, but then *she was yer wife ! !*"

Another protest against this time on violence against women.

other's company and the mood was relaxed. But Amelia had enjoyed
quite a number of men's company in her short life (she was only 24), and
as she went out back to go to the toilet outside she met one of her former
male friends, a man called Amos White. In the reports of what happened
next, he is referred to as an 'old friend', but there was a deep rancour in
their relationship and it is important for the story.

White put a hand on her and was becoming a little too friendly, so
Amelia called for help and of course Johnson came running from the
bar to assist her. The men began to fight. Johnson was not going to lose
in the encounter and he ran off, only to return shortly with a gun in his
hands.

Johnson wasted no time in finding his victim, going directly to him
and firing the shotgun at his chest. White did not take a long time to
die; bystanders grabbed the killer and wrestled him to the ground.
There was no difficulty in having him taken into custody. This all

comes together as a simple story of a man going to violent and deadly extremes to settle a score.

Johnson, at Armley gaol, had the misfortune to be a client of Askern. In fact, he was Askern's last client. On 3 April 1877 he was to hang the Bradford killer, and six reporters were allowed into the event. It was not one of the hangman's better days; at the first attempt the rope broke and Johnson fell to the ground. A black cloth was thrown over the struggling man, and a clergyman prayed loudly for him. The report the next day in *The Times* was as follows: 'While the chaplain was praying that faith and fortitude might be granted to the poor wretch during this horrible interval, search was made for another and surer rope. After a lapse of about ten minutes a new and thicker rope was fastened to the cross beam, and Johnson was led from beneath the drop. With wonderful firmness he re-ascended the fourteen steps of the scaffold. The white cap yet obscured his face, but it did not prevent his voice being audible in prayer. The fresh noose was soon adjusted about his neck, and the fatal bolt again withdrew.'

Even at this second attempt to send him to his Maker, there was an error; it took five minutes for him to die, struggling on the end of the rope. It is amazing that Askern was not immediately sacked.

£50 Damages after a Dog Bite

In 1863, Bradford County Court heard the case of Barden versus Haigh, a story of an attack by a dog. On 6 December 1862, Barden had been playing dominoes with a certain George Hinton at the Old George and Dragon inn in Westgate. When a woman nudged Hinton and spoiled the board, there was a fight. Barden got to his feet to protect the woman, who was about to be punched, and as he did so Haigh's dog bit his leg.

It was a very painful wound and made him ill for several days, so much so that he was unable to work. Eventually he was taken to the infirmary and was there for nine weeks, and so severe was the state of the leg that surgeons wanted to amputate, but the plaintiff in the case would not submit to this. It emerged that this dog had a 'record', as it had previously bitten a child in the face. There was a pathetic attempt in court to claim that the dog did not belong to Haigh, but in the end the judge gave Barden costs and a sum of 50 pounds.

Highway Robbery?

In the mid-Victorian years, as we have seen from the garrotting craze, it was not often safe to walk abroad at night or to travel without company. In 1860 a Mr Joseph Savile alleged that he had been attacked and robbed while going along the Thornton Road at 11 o'clock at night. Savile said he knew his two assailants, fellow pit men James Jennings and William Shaw, claiming that at Well Heads he met the two men and Jennings grabbed his legs while Shaw held his head, and they had thrown him to the ground and then kicked him.

Savile said that he got to his feet and ran away but that they followed, threatening to take his life; he said that he jumped over a wall and crawled to the safety of the darkness. But unfortunately there were no witnesses, and the two defendants told another tale. Witnesses for the accused said that Savile had been very drunk that night, but did say that Savile had been in a fight and that his coat had been ripped. They also said that all Savile had done was tear his coat, and go in a drunken state to his father's house to rant about the coat.

The judge, realising that one side had witnesses and the other did not, stopped the case and the two men were acquitted. The collier's drunken reputation lost the day for him.

A highwayman. (Drawing from an old print.)

FOURTEEN

Forster and his Education Act

'Now we must educate our masters.'

Robert Lowe

By 1870, as research has shown, a large proportion of English working people had a basic standard of literacy. There had been a range of schooling options open to the working-class family, from church controlled to small-scale concerns run locally by various foundations for the improvement of literacy. With this in mind, perhaps W.E. Forster's Education Act of 1870 is not quite as momentous as it was once considered, but still this achievement by a man who became MP for the city and who had established links with the city from 1841 until his death in 1886, is a magnificent one.

There is still a great deal of discussion about just how much reading and writing went on among the lower classes in Victorian Britain. Certainly there was a burgeoning of the popular press in the period and most people were surrounded by written texts; the census returns and marriage certificates are some kind of guide, as are the local studies done on circulating libraries, where numbers of books borrowed may be studied. But the problem is that many of the official forms needed only a signature or a few learned words; they do not necessarily reflect a high level of ability with language.

Nevertheless, the sons and daughters of the lower middle class and the children of the manual workers were certainly in need of a better education; many left school at 11 or 12 anyway, so their need for education was not considered to be intense by many people in society at the time. Something had to be done about the way that schooling was organised and funded, and Forster was to address that.

More than the Education Man

In his long political career, Forster took part in many of the controversies of his time, and took on all kinds of responsibilities and, indeed, political office, being chief secretary for Ireland in Gladstone's 1880 administration. He was born on 11 July 1818, the only son of William Forster of Bradpole in Dorset. He was brought up a Quaker and his first step out in life after school was nowhere near Bradford and had nothing to do with education, because he began in Norwich, where he was involved in hand-loom camlet making. In 1838 he absorbed some knowledge of textiles in a position at Darlington and in 1841 he came to Bradford.

In his life he was to engage with several important issues. Notably there was a radical at the core of him, albeit a theoretical one, for he met the great socialist Robert Owen and even had some sympathy with the less aggressive element in Chartism. He was only in his late 20s when the terrible potato blight struck in Ireland and the years of famine ensued; Forster went to the scene of the disaster and with the Quakers was busy helping to raise money to ease the sufferings of the rural farm workers, notably in Connemara.

He married well, making Jane, the daughter of the famous Thomas Arnold of Rugby School, his wife in 1850 and they were a happy couple. But she would not have seen that much of him because Forster went in for politics in a way that suggests a driven, very ambitious personality. First he stood for Leeds but failed, and then he became Liberal member for Bradford in 1861, and was to hold that position until his death in 1886. In 1865 he had his first important role, as Under Secretary to the Colonies with Cardwell, the army reformer, as his superior. Forster came to know some of the features of the worst side of British colonialism at that point, as he was part of the management group engaged in resolving the severe riots in Jamaica, and then later he was more recognisably the man who brought about the Education Act. He played a major part in bringing about the 1867 Suffrage Act, a piece of legislation which helped to bring the vote to many more people than the 1832 Act.

Education takes Centre Stage

By 1858 there were 21 million children going to school in Britain. Both church charity and family involvement had contributed to this massive increase – an extra 10 million in the preceding 25 years. There had been small steps taken to ensure that workers had a basic education in the century before the 1870 Act. Ragged schools had started in the 1780s, and religious denominations had supplied Sunday Schools; in addition, working-class families were paying fees to cover school costs. Even in the mills, from the 1830s, a little schooling had been built into the early Factory Acts.

Then, in 1861, the Newcastle Commission provided a very important report on the state of education in England; the writers saw that payments of direct grants to schools was the core of the system and that it worked, and that the Government should continue and intensify that kind of support. They found that around one child in eight attended some kind of school and that we were one of the better countries in Europe in that respect.

Forster's aim in his Act was to add to the existing system. The central question was about who should pay for the education of the children in the hugely increased working population – the voluntary bodies or his newly created School Boards? He put the onus on the new boards, and his main measures were these: a division of the country into 2,500 school districts, with School Boards in each district, members of these being locally elected. These Boards were to be responsible for examining the educational provision in their area, thus being able to examine the institutions created and maintained by voluntary bodies. The Boards could even build and maintain new schools – all paid for out of the rates – when the need arose. New by-laws could also be created, allowing them to introduce fee-paying schools if they wished.

Women Involved in the Boards

One of the most remarkable features of Forster's Act was the openings made for women to vote for the School Boards; this meant that women were also candidates for those positions, and of course the new feminist movement could at once understand the importance of their being active in this context. In 1870 there were four women elected to Boards: Flora Stevenson, Lydia Becker, Emily Davies and Elizabeth Garrett.

One Suffragette, writing in 1911, gave an account of School Board elections as they took place in the year of the Forster Act: 'In the first School

Board election, which took place in London in November, 1870, Miss Elizabeth Garrett and Miss Emily Davies were returned as members. Miss Garrett was at the head of the poll in her constituency – Marylebone. She polled more than 47,000 votes, the largest number, which had ever been bestowed upon any candidate in any election in England.'

But there were some dissenting voices against Forster's Act. The Non-conformists were not happy and were disillusioned with Gladstone's Government. In contrast, the role taken by church schools was integrated and seen as important, and to be preserved.

If we spin the figures another way, it could be said that just over a million children were in state-aided elementary schools in 1870, out of a population of 4.3 million. Also, there were still two million without educational provision. Attending to the gap in provision was a major project, and it was all about cash: both voluntary and board schools would receive finance, but only the board schools would have the local rate levied; voluntary schools would still rely on their endowments.

There was a schism, as historian Anthony Wood has written: 'Deep sincerity of religious belief led to bitter disputes at the time of elections to the School Boards, and the antagonism was so great that the Boards sometimes hindered the growth of educational institutions in order to spite their rivals.'

What really annoyed so many at the time was the fact that the Boards could decide locally on whether or not there would be any kind of religious instruction in their schools. Such repercussions were bound to create disagreements, but then we have to ask what legislation ever existed which did not create differences of opinion? In Victorian times, when change was fast and furious, measures were often ad hoc and hurried, but at least Forster had planned well and consulted widely.

Ireland

Forster in later life was busy in Ireland; he was working there as Secretary and he had to take on the Land leagues and the Home Rule Party under the charismatic Charles Stewart Parnell. The Land Act of 1870 had failed to attend to the power of the landlords, and made it possible for a tenant to be evicted without any payment of compensation. Matters were very unsettled and Forster was in the middle of a tough confrontation and, when Parnell was released from prison by Gladstone, Forster resigned. He had been given

Forster Square - well before recent developments.

the nickname 'Buckshot' Forster, which he gained when he gave the order that Irish police were to have their weapons loaded with buckshot rather than with the more lethal ball cartridge. It seems strange that Forster began to be seen as a hard-liner and a relentless authoritarian when in fact his buckshot measure was done through care and concern for the Irish people.

Forster's life was threatened at the time, and he was attacked in Parliament. His resignation was also down to the sheer fatigue he had suffered, as well as the principle regarding Parnell. In April 1882, after Parnell's release, Forster's resignation may well have been due to tiredness as well as disillusion.

Forster died in London on 5 April 1886. It has to be recalled that, as well as these national and international affairs, Forster was concerned with issues and events on his own doorstep in Bradford. In keeping with his zeal for popular education, he made reading rooms for the public and arranged for 'works trips', as in the trip to London for over 500 of his employees in 1862. He was a joint-owner of Greenholme Mills in Burley-in-Wharfedale, and had made great progress in local business since his first business, a partnership with William Fison at Waterloo Mills in Market Street.

Of course, his name is there in Forster Square, along with the statue. Arguably, Bradford had one of the most successful and enterprising School Boards in the 1890s, under the guidance of Margaret McMillan, whose innovations included free school meals and milk. Forster would have approved.

FIFTEEN

Samuel Cunliffe Lister

'It was never intended that young Samuel would become a tradesman...'

William Scruton

Arguably, Titus Salt and Samuel Cunliffe Lister could be described as the giants of Bradford history, yet in some important ways they were very different presences in the city and their legacies to Bradford provide sharp and marked contrasts. Salt was the exemplar of the local philanthropist and benefactor; Lister tended to be an absentee, and bought huge tracts of land in North Yorkshire. It was said of Lister that he was better informed about the economics of the United States of America than he was about the Bradford woollen workers.

But there is no doubt that Lister, born at Calverley Hall on 1 January 1815, was a truly remarkable man in an era of remarkable men: he was the fourth son of Ellis Cunliffe, and was intended for ordination and a career in the church, as younger

Cunliffe Lister.
(From Scruton's *Pen and Pencil Sketches of Old Bradford*.)

sons of the wealthy usually were at that time. But he was keen on business, and in 1838 with his elder brother John he had a mill bought for him by his father and a chance to build and go forward in the local industry. He was educated at a private school in Clapham and was given a first commercial post in Liverpool, but Bradford was his destination and, at only 21, he was at Manningham Hall and ready to enter the business world in earnest. His brother was to die while they were in partnership in their mill, leaving Samuel to lead the business himself – clearly something he was more than capable of doing. His business acumen and his inventor's mind burgeoned in parallel.

Lister was destined to be very rich and successful, and in the world of invention as well as in business.

One of the Modern Millionaires

In 1890 James Burnley, the Bradford writer, included Lister in a long essay on modern millionaires and he explained Lister's work in this way: 'Mr. S. C. Lister, the Bradford "Silk King" is another living example of the trade millionaire. Like Mr Holden, he was early interested in the invention of wool-combing machinery; indeed his was the leading name in this branch of industry for many years, and he was receiving £1,000 a machine before Mr Holden came on the scene as a woolcomber; but the climax of his ingenuity and success was his utilisation of silk waste…His merited reward has been an income monarchs might envy…'

Mention of Isaac Holden reminds us that Lister and Holden had an acrimonious period of competition regarding who actually had claims for particular patents in the wool-combing mechanisation which went ahead steadily as the century wore on.

Lister was described in his lifetime as having 'a wonderful aptitude for business, an indomitable perseverance, and sheer strength of will…'

Patents and Silk Waste

When he applied his brain and expertise to the problems of wool-combing, he spent years improving the existing machines and then made sure that he took out patents for his inventions; he also bought up the patents of rivals and the demand for his machines showed such intensity that what cost him £200 was sold for £1,200.

Lister's Mill, close up. By Laura Carter.

In exploiting the waste products from the silk spinning industry, Lister showed that typical Victorian attitude of universal utility: waste nothing and make pounds from pennies. He worked hard and invested massive sums of money in developing a machine that would be capable of using the silk waste to produce a new product, and of course that investment paid off very well. Silk-combing machines were eventually made, and he could then produce yarn that cost sixpence a pound and sell it for 23 shillings a pound. He also made a loom for the treatment of velvet piled fabrics, and this silk production made his wealth: the work at Manningham Mill gave him an annual income of £200,000. His company could produce carpets and poplins and even synthetic sealskins.

Because the rate of production therefore increased, there was a new demand for more raw wool and so, as a consequence of his endeavours, wool from Australia was imported.

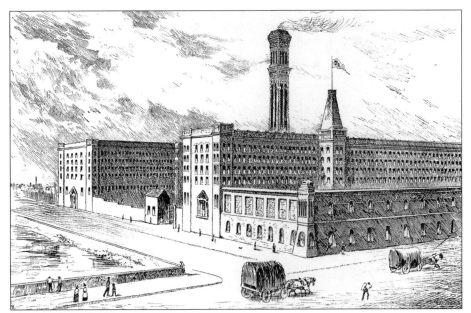

Manningham Mills. (Burnley's *Romance of Modern Industry*, 1890.)

Public Life and Wealth – and a Strike

Lister had plenty of money with which to invest in land, and he bought extensive estates at Jervaulx and Middleham; he was to be created Lord Masham in 1891, taking that title as a reference to the town close to his land at Swinton Park. He acted as a Justice of the Peace for both the North Riding and the West Riding and also later became a county High Sheriff. His many inventions finally won him other honours, notably the award of the Albert Medal in 1886. He received most of the honours normally given to celebrated local heroes: Freeman of the city and a statue in Lister Park. In spite of that fact, he never became Mayor of Bradford, something that happened to most of the local businessmen who succeeded on a large scale.

Perhaps the only real negative event in his business life was the bitter Manningham strike of 1890–91. This was one of those occasions on which the mayor of Bradford actually had to read the Riot Act; some

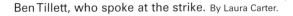

Ben Tillett, who spoke at the strike. By Laura Carter.

'Modern Millionaries'. (Burnley's *Romance of Modern Industry*, 1890.)

SIR TITUS SALT.   GEORGE MOORE.
                    LORD ARMSTRONG.
        S. CUNLIFFE LISTER.   ISAAC HOLDEN.

thought there was a hex on the place, as one mill on the site had been burned down in 1873 and there was extreme violence and mobs on the rampage. The riot was the culmination of a 19-week strike, and it is hard to believe that a crowd of 3,000 people gathered for an illegal meeting, a spin-off from the speeches made by leading radicals to the workers concerned in the Manningham strike, and perhaps even more stunning, after a period of unrest and violence, the Durham Light Infantry charged the crowd.

Lister Park

In 1870, Lister sold Manningham Park to Bradford Corporation for £40,000 – just half of what it was worth. On 18 August that year, the park was opened to the public. Today, the park has an art gallery, sports facilities and a lake, but when Lister was there it was his home, and after selling the land he moved to Farfield Hall at Addingham. He was not content to simply have the park, however, and in 1898 he planned to build Cartwright Memorial Hall there. That building was completed in 1904.

Royalty came to Bradford in May after the opening of the hall, and there was a Bradford version of the Great Exhibition put on, to show off

Cartwright Hall with guard of honour.

the products, skills and expertise of the city's artisans. The park became the people's park and as time went on it became a favourite location for local people for all kinds of leisure pursuits. Everything we think of when we bring to mind Edwardian Sunday recreation applies to Lister Park: bandstands, family walks, even gondolas and launches on the lake; local people have a treasure-house of memories of seeing strikingly unusual sights there, such as a model of a massive steam locomotive on one occasion and, on another, a 'palace of illusions'.

Samuel Cunliffe Lister lived a long and productive life, dying at the age of 91 in February 1906 at home in Swinton Park. He will be remembered for many things, and one of the least acknowledged of these is the fact that he was the first Member of Parliament elected for Bradford after the great 1832 Reform Act.

SIXTEEN

James Burnley: Saunterer

'Amongst the leading poets of Yorkshire, the name of James Burnley occupies a prominent position...'

William Andrews

One of the most fascinating studies in local history relates to questions of region and belonging. We cannot resist this pull of curiosity about how and why our ancestors expressed their identity through such aspects of popular culture as local dialect literature, songs, parades, concerts and so on. In the Victorian period this curiosity is perhaps more easily explained. After all, this was the period of turmoil and rapid social change in which issues of class difference became more acute and significant.

In the late 19th century there was a widespread flowering of local writing, often in the vernacular, and sometimes in remarkably original and vibrant dialect. It was a period in which local and regional publishing was developing, and it was not difficult for an earnest middle-class amateur poet to bring his or her work into print. The sense of local belonging was mediated to all classes, however, and the literature of the time shows the awareness on the part of the publishers that they should cater for all tastes.

The Bradford Setting

It is in Bradford, perhaps, more than in any other Yorkshire Victorian city, that the literary culture around the new aspirations of reading and writing both high-quality literature and popular narratives is apparent.

There are many reasons for this: the influx of German immigrants who brought their love of higher cultural pursuits, the appeal of a bohemian, cosmopolitan culture to the new middle class and, most of all, to the energy of individuals. In Bradford there was a 'nest of singing birds' (as Dr Johnson described his literary coterie) gathered around various clubs, coffee houses and societies, and a key figure in this was the writer and journalist James Burnley.

The time was right for such a figure to emerge. The local civic pride was developing in step with the legislation for incorporation (Bradford being made a County Borough in 1889) and with the establishment of literary and philosophical societies such as those thriving in Leeds and Hull in the mid-Victorian years. As Asa Briggs puts it when comparing Leeds and Bradford: 'Bradford was the first of the two communities to sponsor a handsome new public building which was designed to "elevate" taste and meet the cultural needs of a business metropolis' and also, with St George's Hall, Briggs points out, 'What happened inside it was to raise the tone of society also.'

A fundamental part of this Bradford culture, though, was in the people, not simply in the buildings and grand public gestures of politicians. Writing was becoming a booming local cultural product, offering outlets for the mediocre enthusiast as well as the genuine creative spirit. James Burnley was at the heart of this, as editor, poet, comedian and serious social commentator. As Ian Dewhirst has pointed out, the authors being published could range from clergymen to anonymous operatives from the factory floor. Burnley came on the literary scene with a few poems and a knowledge of the London theatre in the 1860s, and soon became involved with the group of writers around the *Bradford Observer* and the *Bradford Review*.

Several writers of later years have commented on the cultural richness and diversity of late Victorian Bradford, so it is not difficult to imagine the context in which Burley thrived. W. Riley, for instance, in his autobiography, notes: 'Good reference libraries were close at hand; good lectures were available; cultured men and women were ready to stimulate and encourage the serious student. As I recall to mind the opportunities that then presented themselves, I appropriate to myself the well-known line of Wordsworth "Bliss was it in that dawn to be alive".'

Peter Holdsworth has pointed out the importance of this setting for the young J.B. Priestley, commenting that '...in his youth Bradford was...culturally dynamic. Theatre, literary pursuits, sport and the visual arts thrived alongside a host of societies.'

The Saunterer

However, in the earlier period, when Burnley arrived, there was a notable difference to the more institutionalised developments of *fin de siècle* Bradford. The writing was more directly comprehensive, aware of what working men wanted in their reading, as well as supplying reading matter for the middle class. Burnley had such a wide range of writing ability that he could fit in with the drinkers and workers at Thomas Nicholson's eating house in Kirkgate, talking to almanac writers and singers, but also dining with the large-scale entrepreneurs whose lives he was to write about in his best-selling book, *The Romance of Modern Industry* (1886).

Burnley was born in Shipley in 1842 and began his long publishing career with a volume of poems, *Idonia and Other Poems* (1869), but his

Saunterer's Satchel.

SAUNTERER'S SATCHEL.

TO MY READERS.

Another year's come round, and here again I'm found my Satchel wide revealing. My wares are all brand new, and open to your view without the least concealing. I bring some fancy bits—a few artistic hits—by way of illustration; I'm sure they'll give your eyes agreeable surprise, and get your commendation. So take this new collection, and give it kind inspection—it's all I have to-day—and when the next year comes I'll bring fresh threads and thrums, so please be in the way.

OWD NIVVERSWEAT AN' HIS HORSE.

Pool thy chair up, lad, an I'll tell tha all abaht it. It com abaht i' this way. Ahr Sam hed been ovver into Belgium on a cheap trip—one o' them trips whear they Cook for 'em, thah knaws—an he'd seen some famous strong Flemish horses. He said they wor as big as a cah an as strong as a elephant, an nowt ud dew bud we mud hev one. I'm not mitch of a lover o' furrin stuff myseln, thah knaws, bud we'd a varry deeal o' heavy leadin on just then, an I thowt if theaze Flemish horses really wor as strong as Sam said they wor, it ud happen be as weel if we gat one. So we let owd Bengdrop, t'horse dealer, knaw 'at we wanted one, an i' less nor a fortnit he gat one for us reyt direct aht o' Belgium, an we paid him a stiff price for it an all. Thah nivver saw sitch a horse i' thy life, ta lewk at. It wor as thick rahnd t'body as a engine boiler, an wor varry uppish i' t'hinnd pairt—summat like a camel wi' t'hump thrawn rayther ta far back—an it hed a heead as big as a cham'er door. "Well," says I, " thah may be able ta pool a bit, bud whether ta can or nut thah'rt a fahl un." Ivverybody 'at saw it brast aht o' laffin at it, an I don't think Sam bizsen altogether liked t'lewk on't. Hahsumivver, we gat it into t'stable an let it rest itsenn a bit, an it did rest an all. It laid itsenn dahn like a gurt hippopotamus an nivver stirred for monny a bahr. Sam kept goin ta lewk at it, an kept tryin ta get it ta eyt summat, bud it woddant stir a wedge. It seemed as if it nivver meant to get up no more. "There's summat ails this horse," says Sam, when he'd gettan reyt wearied aht. "Theer's summat ails thee I'm beginnin ta think," I says, " or thah'd nivver ha hed thy heead turned wi a lump o' furrin muck like that. Dash it," I says, "thah'rt as bad as t'vicar wife; shoo nivver thinks shoo can get a bonnet fit ta put on nuless it comes throo Paris, an e goy shoo's awlus biggest freet i' t'church." Sam said nowt to this, bud he scratted his heead an began o' lewkin dahn i' t'mahth. After a while he says, "I think it wants physicin." "Aw, varry weel," I says, "let's physic it then." So I got two pund an a bawf o' castor oil, an it tewk it like new milk. Then we gat six pund o' linseed an made it a bucketful o' gruel, an mixed a pund o' ginger in't.

talents extended to other compositions such as plays, sketches, travel writing, fiction and journalism. He became most celebrated as 'The Saunterer', the man who produced the almanac *The Saunterer's Satchel* throughout the last decades of the century, and was also well known for his 'sketches books' – *Phases of Bradford Life* (1871) and *West Riding Sketches* (1875). These two books illustrate the special qualities that made Burnley central to this Bradford literary culture: his mix of serious commentary and accessible humour, and his ability to embrace the range of cultural reference from folklore to modern industrial processes. In fact, his most successful books celebrated the woollen industry and the wider Victorian preoccupations with 'rags to riches' themes in the age of Samuel Smiles and his phenomenal best-seller *Self-Help* (1859). His book *The History of Wool and Wool-Combing* (1889) appears to have made his name nationally and gave him access to the drawing-rooms of the wealthy.

Burnley and his Journals

What defines Burnley's importance to Bradford writing and to the massive success of the whole group of journalists and poets around him are his local publishing achievements, largely with the founding of *The Yorkshireman* in 1875, initially as a monthly. In later years, as one memoirist puts it, he resided in London 'and made a host of friends among the leading literati of the metropolis'. In other words, here we have a writer who was one of a class who succeeded in the wake of the huge ocean liner that was dominating the age – the shrine of 'Literature' – and Burnley was a 'bookman' in that context, one of the smaller vessels perhaps, to follow the metaphor.

For the student of Yorkshire writing, his importance is illustrated when we look closer at the nature of the almanac *The Saunterer's Satchel*. Here was a publication that stands out in its time. The almanac, as established in the working-class author tradition, notably in Barnsley, Halifax and Leeds, had been primarily a calendar with anniversaries and local adverts (notably of patent medicines) and perhaps the first type of popular publication supplying local dialect verse and narrative that provided sustenance for the local and civic pride so evident at the time. The most celebrated almanac, John Hartley's *Clock Almanac*, exemplifies this. An

Penny readings – one of the many popular volumes for clubs and groups.

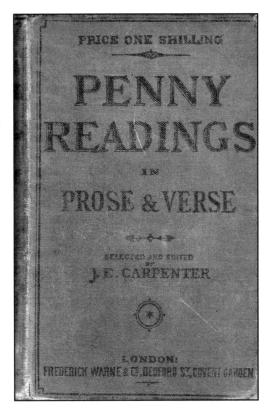

average issue would contain humour, anecdotes and rhymes, all very much to the popular taste and similar to the material in demand for penny readings and for dialect recitals such as those given by Ben Preston following afternoon tea and Bible classes. The success of penny readings was obviously a factor. London publishers were producing hardback volumes for these readings by the 1870s, notably Frederick Warne.

Burnley's *Satchel* is something else completely. A typical issue would contain a preface with a chatty tone, a comic drama set in Yorkshire, songs and rhymes in dialect and in standard English, and fiction. Burnley also introduced an *Answers to Correspondents* column and local news. These were to continue in the more ambitious *Yorkshireman*. But what defines the difference between the *Satchel* and its competitors are the literary allusions and parodies it included. For instance, we have 'A Kersmas tale – not by Munchausen' and rhymes 'not by Poe'. In one rhyme, 'Sing the Song of the Fleece' Burnley calls the sections of the poem 'fyttes', so referring to some mediaeval forms. All this indicates that his readership was a mix of the people who simply wanted racy and farcical tales and the middle-class aspirants who read 'good literature' and would know a parody when they read it. Even more impressive was the local and topographical nature of the references squeezed into the rhymes, such as 'Of Alpacas superb in which Salts are investors/Of the fleece of the goat from the wilds of Angora/which makes such sweet dresses for Florry and Dora.'

Literary recollections

The contents and tone of *The Satchel* indicate that Burnley was keenly aware of the readership, and that the keynote was entertainment. Repeatedly, his prefaces stress the content as being 'puns, quite a sea for jokers facetious to dabble in' and 'stories fantastic and stories sarcastic.' His aim is always to promote writers 'who've been rangers in regions sublime, whose pens, by heaven nourished, give forth grand thoughts for all time.' In a remarkable typescript written by Burnley in later life, *Literary Recollections of Bradford 1870–1890*, he summarises the groups of literati around the city at the time. These would be the writers who supplied copy to the whole range of magazines, almanacs and journals of the area. Burnley lists the main figures: '...and into this haunt would occasionally stray for mind-communion John James, the historian of Bradford, for he frequently visited the town he had made famous; Robert Storey, the Craven poet, Ben Preston, Stephen Fawcett, James Hird and others, with mine host Nicholson, smoking his long pipe and presiding...'

In his book *Phases of Bradford Life*, in which Burnley collected many of his local writings, he has a piece on 'Coffee House Life' and this makes clear exactly what it was like to be involved in this 'mind communion': 'Here in Bradford there still exist coffee rooms where discussion on the topics of the day constitute a special feature, and where almost any night may be heard debates equal in vigour, if not in ability, to any heard within the walls of the House of Commons.'

He writes of 'Straycock's Temperance Hotel' in a dingy court off Kirkgate, and has gentle fun at the expense of a crowd of regulars. Even more pastiche and satire are injected into a sketch called 'Barnacle's Evening Party,' in which Dickens's Pickwick Club is echoed. The guest list is an exaggeration of the range of writers who perhaps really did gather in the Bradford writers' circles of the age. They include such worthies as 'Abimelech Flavonius de Smithkins, the great local author and historian of Wibsey Slack' and 'Mr Silvanio, the tragedian'. Barnacles provides his guests with a selection of literature for the party, and this includes 'Long yarns by an Old Spinner – a most amusing volume' and 'Looming in the distance – a three-volume novel by the author of *Fell'd at Last*.'

There were some remarkable characters in the circle around Burnley, and their enthusiasm and high level of literary appreciation is typified by

J. Arthur Binns, whom Burnley describes in this way: 'He was…A man of some leisure and disclosed to me a mind better stored with literary knowledge than that of any man I have ever known…He was chairman of the library committee of the old Mechanics' Institute. He knew the poets so thoroughly that he had many of their best pieces literally off by heart. He could recite the whole of Pope's *Essay on Man* and reel off poems and stanzas by Shelley…'

To Bradford generally, Binns was known as the president of the Third Equitable Building Society.

Burnley was always hankering after a bohemian literary life and a Yorkshire Literary Union was formed in April 1870. Burnley recalled, 'It must not be imagined that the Bradford writers did not chum together socially as well as in literary matters…There was a strain of Bohemianism about some of us…'

He clearly hankered for a mix of café society and serious literary production, and his works reflect this diversity.

His Achievement

Burnley's work in Bradford has a greater significance than has been given to him. As a writer, propagandist for social progress and the amelioration of man through work and cultural fulfilment, Burnley surely deserves to be re-read. His writings provide valuable evidence of important social and cultural history, but far more important than that is his place in the chronicles of both an emerging working-class interest in literature and in the middle-class acquisition of their own cultural values in the acceptance of civic pride and local belonging. All this came at a time when English literature was only just in the process of becoming recognised as a subject with meaning and status. But it was the Bradford setting, and its unique contributions to the new

Jerome K. Jerome, one of Burnley's associates.

publishing enterprises that gave Burnley his real break as a writer. As he puts it in the introduction to *West Riding Sketches*: 'In the West Riding...the old and new clash together so indiscriminately, the prose and the poetry intermingle so curiously, that it requires one to be native and to the manor born to distinguish the lines of demarcation.'

Burnley was very much the creation of that growth of regional consciousness born of civic pride, and the writers in his circle certainly understood that Yorkshire was an entity, as part of a concept of 'The North', that it was also a state of mind, and that it needed a literature of its own, largely to counteract the stereotypes given to places north of the Trent by London writers.

In helping to cultivate these things in and around Bradford, Burnley was more than simply a jobbing literary man. He and his Bradford friends never produced anything that did not have its foundations in an affection for the city and the immediate countryside. In the final words of his memoir, he wrote: 'Of course, every decade does not give Bradford a Ben Preston or a Broughton, or a Robbins...still, with the encouraging examples of those twenty years to look back upon, there ought to be incentive enough to budding literary talent to put forth its highest endeavours in advancing the literary reputation of this good old town.'

How right he was. In the decade after Burnley's time there, a young J.B. Priestley was talking shop in the Swan Arcade and reading the almanacs.

A study of James Burnley's achievement in Bradford surely confirms for us the importance of looking again at figures like him, people who valued the talent on their own patch and did everything to encourage it.

SEVENTEEN

Miss Gertie Millar and Mr John Coates

We Never do that in Yorkshire
One of Gertie's hit songs

Bradford has a long and rich tradition of music and musical theatre, and the city can boast a long line of celebrities in popular song, musicals and in classical music. These two performers represent that feature of Bradford: Millar in comedy and song, and Coates in the world of light entertainment. They symbolise in some ways the simple pleasures of 'a night out' or a matinee in the days long before television and mass communications.

Gertie's Beginnings

Gertrude Millar was born on 20 February 1879, in a street near Carlisle Road; later, her family settled in Drewton Street. Gertie went to school at Christ Church, very near her Drewton Street home. There is no doubt that she would have seen the Theatre Royal every day, and her dreams of fame on the stage must have been kindled at a very young age.

In her obituary in 1952, it was written that 'Gossip in her heyday said that she had been a mill-hand and worn the clogs…' But her talent was spotted early on and she appeared in *The Babes in the Wood* at the St James' Theatre in Manchester at the tender age of 13. After that she moved into pantomime, notably playing Dandini in *Cinderella* at the Grand Theatre in Fulham. But she was also working in Bradford, booked by Walter Holmes for St George's Hall. Her talent for comedy was

Miss Gertie Millar.

especially seen and developed, and it did not take long for Gertie to be appearing in the West End, where it was at the Gaiety Theatre that she really made her name. She had started in John Hart's child pantomimes and moved within a few years to the 'big stage' of London.

Gaiety, Lionel Monckton and New York

When Gertie was playing in *The Messenger Boy* she was watched by Lionel Monckton, the composer of the major hit *The Arcadians*. Lionel was impressed and also fell in love with her. Their story together began with an immediate affection and they were very soon married. Monckton teamed up with Ivan Caryll to write the music for *The Toreador*, produced by George Edwardes at the Gaiety. Gertie played the bridesmaid in that production – the character of Cora Bellamy – and the press made a big hit out of 'Captivating Cora'. A star was born.

She was at the Gaiety for seven years, but that included her appearance at the new theatre of that name, built by Edwardes, and she was in the opening production of *The Orchid* in 1903. Monckton and Caryll had become a successful writing team by then and they delighted in writing pieces for her own brand of comedy; one of the first songs in that genre was *Oh Take Care of Little Mary* – inspired by a play of J.M. Barrie's. Other hits followed, including *The Spring Chicken* and *The Girls of Gottenburg*.

In 1908 she went to work at what was then the Hicks Theatre (later the Globe) because the great operetta composer, Oscar Strauss, wanted her for *A Waltz Dream*. This did very well indeed, and so, paired with her hit *The Girls of Gottenburg*, she went across the Atlantic to woo the theatre-goers of New York. Again she did so, and her reputation was growing fast. But in 1909 her Bradford roots played a part in her work, as she had a big hit with *We Never do that in Yorkshire* and then with her most well known song, *I'm such a Silly when the Moon Comes Out*. Of all these activities, it is *The Orchid* that stands out: she played the role in that production for 559 performances, and then later almost as many times in *The Quaker Girl* in 1910. It was hard for a singer in those days to avoid a Franz Lehar work and, sure enough, Gertie appeared in *Gipsy Love* in the summer of 1912, possibly her busiest year, because later she was in Monckton's *The Dancing Mistress* and also in a revival of *The*

Country Girl. Lionel Monckton had that special rapport with her that led to her most loved songs and they had the nation singing and humming with his *Neville was a Devil* in 1915.

A typical Gertie Millar number was the duet she sang with Edmund Payne in *The Girls of Gottenburg*. This was *Two Little Sausages* and this is a sample of the kind of humour:

'Once in a window of a ham and beef shop
Two little sausages sat.
One was a lady and one was a gentleman
Sausages are like that!
He fell a victim to her simple charm
And her form he would have embraced.
But a sausage, you see, never has any arm,
And the lady hadn't got a waist...'

But the affection for Gertie's brand of musical comedy was declining in the war years, and her last appearance in London was in *Flora* at the Prince of Wales Theatre in 1918. By then she was almost retired, though she did appear at the Alhambra in a revue.

A Dash of Scandal

One event that rocked this seemingly happy and successful life and marriage was the death of Baron Gunther Rau von Holzhausen, whose body was found in Gertie's boudoir in Russell Square, Bloomsbury, in November 1905. *The Times* reported on the inquest, held at St Pancras Coroner's Court: 'Kate Ferrell, servant to Mr Lionel Monckton, deposed that on entering Mrs Monckton's boudoir shortly after seven o'clock on Sunday morning she noticed that one of the window panes was broken. In stooping to pick up the broken glass behind the piano, which stood diagonally in one corner, she noticed a man's feet, and hurried out to acquaint Mr Monckton. As she did so she heard the report of a firearm. Access to the room by the window could easily be obtained from the street.'

Witnesses confirmed the general impression that the Baron was a sad case: he had been gambling heavily at the races and drinking, and was in a depressed state after writing romantic letters to Gertie, knowing that she could never reciprocate. The night before the death, the Baron had been

Russell Square, where the Baron entered and shot himself.

in the stalls watching Gertie, and he had arranged for a note to be handed to her as she left the stage. We will never know what the note was, but it seems likely that it hinted at his suicide.

Gertie made a deposition at the inquest, saying that she had known the Baron for about 18 months and that she had 'treated him as a friend'. The Baron and a lady friend had dined with the Moncktons on one occasion. One factor in his sad condition may have been that he had suffered a severe blow in an accident when he had fallen from his horse about a month before his death. She said he had written to her, saying he was 'destitute and utterly tired'. Gertie had told him that their friendship would have to end – he was trying to push things into a romantic liaison and he was fantasising about the relationship. He had done all the usual things such as sending letters and flowers, but Gertie was adamant in saying that she had never dined alone with the baron.

The police officer who came to the scene, Constable William O'Connor, said that when he came to Russell Square, he saw the Baron crouching behind the piano, called to him, and then the constable approached and saw that the man had shot himself in the temple.

The End – and a Celebration!

Gertie Millar died in April 1952, and by that time she was a countess, as she had married Walter Humble Ward, Earl of Dudley, shortly after the death of Lionel Monckton in 1924. Ward died in 1932, and so Gertie had 20 years alone, living in France and then later back in Britain, dying in Chiddingford, Surrey.

Two years before her death, the musical world paid tribute to her and to the old Gaiety. This took place in the dining room of the Dorchester Hotel and one report said that '...there was no denying the magic by which the spirit of the Gaiety itself – the old Gaiety Theatre in the Strand – was invoked and some of its famous names called into the charmed circle.'

Gertie Millar was there, and she appeared to take a bow and enjoy the applause. The band played tunes from her hit *Our Miss Gibbs* and former stars blew kisses to the audience. As the writer of that event put it at the time, 'Musical comedy was invented for the Gaiety.' As for the Bradford lass, she stood among the presences of such names at Sarah Bernhardt,

Ruby Miller, Clare Romaine, Ivor Novello and Lupino Lane. *The Times* reported after the celebration that 'In tens of thousands of homes would be found an old Gaiety programme, or a photograph of one of the girls...' She was one of the first Bradford singers to move in that world, but she would not be the last.

John Coates

In 1900 at the Steinway Hall, it was reported that at the International Ballad Concert, 'Mr John Coates sang Coleridge-Taylor's charming song, *Sweet Evenings Come and Go, Love* with much taste and gave full effect to Sullivan's *Take a Pair of Sparkling Eyes*.' That says a lot about the Bradford-born singer's versatility and panache. He was steadily popular, a regular tenor in all kinds of contexts if a song was needed.

Coates was born on 29 June 1865 and his family lived in Carlisle Place and Girlington Road. He started at Bradford Grammar School at the age of eight and was soon singing both solo and in the choir. After his father died, when John was only 12, he started work in a warehouse office. Amazingly, his courage and sheer sense of adventure made him go to London to forge a singing career at the age of 28. After the usual struggle for the northern lad who goes to the big city in search of a career, he managed to get a break singing with the D'Oyly Carte. He was at first a baritone, but the teacher, William Shakespeare, told him he was a tenor and the change was made to good effect.

Coates managed to find work on tours, both at home in the provinces and abroad. In 1899 he appeared in Bradford, singing *The Absent-Minded Beggar* at the Alhambra. In the Edwardian period, he found a place in the Moody Manners Company and then with Beecham; he toured further afield with these, and steadily established a reputation.

'The Dream of Gerontius'

As one writer said of Coates, his name will always be inseparably linked with Elgar's oratorio, *The Dream of Gerontius*. He sang the title role for the first time at the Worcester Festival in 1902 and that was the true appearance of that great work, something which made its name more widely than before. It was, as a *Times* writer said, 'the launching of his second career as a singer'.

After that, he was much in demand at various festivals around the land, notably in modern oratorio. He sang in Birmingham later, again involved with Elgar's work, but also performing such works as Gavin Bantock's *Omar Khayyam* and, in Leeds, singing Walford Davies' *Everyman*. His wider fame meant that, for example, to German audiences he was 'the English Lohengrin' and he also became a regular performer in Thomas Beecham's Covent Garden events.

Soldier

Coates joined the National Reserve when World War One began in 1914. He was 49 but still keen to do his bit for England, and a man who knew him wrote to *The Times* just after the singer's death to make a point; this was a certain 'L.N.' and he wrote that '...he would not be satisfied until he was a real fighting soldier. As a result of his irrepressible perseverance, he was granted a commission in the Green Howards early in 1915.' Amazingly, at the age of 51, Coates was on active service in France until the end of the war.

The Revd Arthur Dolphin knew Coates as a soldier and he was with him for officer training in Middlesex. Dolphin wrote later: 'I heard him singing while he was taking a shower bath and, having no idea who he was, boldly asked him to sing at a camp concert. He hesitated but later explained matters. He engaged a famous London pianist as his accompanist and gave us a whole evening's recital from Elizabethan music to the latest patriotic song. It remains the most memorable camp concert in my life.'

John Coates began singing again in 1919 and continued his successes, but from the 1930s he became a radio personality. Coates died at Northwood, Middlesex, in August 1941.

EIGHTEEN

Hangman Berry

'I have called hanging brutal because there is nothing romantic or heroic in connection with it…'

Robert Watson

In March 1884 James Berry of Heckmondwike wrote a letter to the prison authorities. He was a former police officer, so his letter related to his past experience, because he was applying to be an executioner. He wrote: 'I most respectfully apply to you, to ask if you will permit me to conduct the execution of the two convicts now lying under sentence of death at Edinburgh. I was very intimate with the late Mr. Marwood…I now have one rope which I bought from him at Horncastle and have had two made from it. I have also two pinioning straps…'

The Marwood he refers to was a Lincolnshire man who had perfected the more humane method of official hanging that made use of the long drop. In other words, he made it possible to kill by quick asphyxiation rather than by the brutal strangulation previously used. He had calculated a drop in accordance with the victim's weight. Berry was keen to step into Marwood's shoes and had learned from the master.

Whether Berry is one of Bradford's heroes or villains is open to question, but the short answer is that in 1884 Britain had a policy of capital punishment within the criminal law and someone had to do it.

Berry and the hanging traditions

Since Saxon times, people had been hanged as a method of judicial death in this country. In early times it was manorial and regional, and into the early 19th century there were still local hangmen employed, as at York. But there was a need for a general public executioner as the Victorian

A hanging of a woman.

period wore on and public executions ended (in 1868). As hangings began to take place inside the prisons with a medley of professional men present, the hangman was expected to be rather more competent than some of his Georgian antecedents. One York hangman called Curry was notorious for taking a drink for some Dutch courage on the day he had to hang someone on the Knavesmire, and he tended to bungle things, so that at times his clients were dangling on the rope, kicking and choking for several minutes.

James Berry was always an eccentric character. Restless, he moved from job to job, but in hanging he found his true vocation. As with many other men in his profession, the reasons for doing that unpleasant work were partly financial and partly related to a notion of 'national moral service'. Undoubtedly it was an occupation that provided a very lucrative second income for a working man; it was always a part-time affair, right up to the end of hanging in 1964. In Berry's case, the attractions were more income for his family, some travel, and a sense that he was ridding the world of villains.

The trade was becoming almost a job with a mystique attached by 1884 when Berry wrote his application and within a few years there was to be a reorganisation of the training of hangmen. In Berry's career most of the time he was quite proficient, with just a few blunders to his name.

Career and Famous Cases

James Berry was born in February 1852, his father Daniel being a wool-stapler. His family were Methodists and would clearly have had a problem applying restraint and morality to young, wild James. He was always in scrapes and very nearly died when struck by a horse; he also ran away to try to have a life on the ocean waves but only reached Goole. But he did have some schooling, despite the fact that he was easily led by various tearaways around him.

As a young adult, he was attracted to the police constabulary and served in Bradford after marrying at Richmond Terrace Chapel, Horton. He did well in the force, but always tended to bear grudges and cause dissension. After a spell in Nottingham and other abortive attempts to change career he settled on coal merchandising, and then the opportunity came along to earn some good money in the hanging trade.

By 1861 there were only two capital offences left on the statute books: treason and murder, but there was plenty of business for Berry. His application went to the Sheriffs of London and Middlesex in 1883 and he was called to interview at the Old Bailey, but he was just beaten to the job by another man, Bartholomew Binns. In the grand tradition of drunks at the scaffold, Binns made some severe mistakes, such as his disgusting bungle of a hanging in Liverpool in 1883. Binns was later fined and disciplined, and finally sacked after another drunken excursion to Liverpool.

Berry was therefore next in line and had powerful references in place; he was in office and set to do his first hanging in Glasgow, where he was to officiate at a double hanging of two poachers.

Berry was to be on the Home Office list of executioners for seven years, from 1884 to 1891, and in that time he executed 131 people. Five of these clients were women, the most harrowing of which was the hanging of Mary Lefley in Lincoln prison in May 1884. She was only the third person he hanged, and the whole affair was most alarming and upsetting for all concerned. Mary constantly protested her innocence of killing her husband and the officials at the prison were also convinced of her innocence. Berry was the first hangman to write any memoirs and he gives a shocking account of the occasion there: 'Imagine my feelings when I went to the condemned cell to prepare her for her doom. I know that my hands trembled as the turnkey held open the door, and my tongue clove to the roof of my mouth as I essayed speech. Mary Lefley was in bed. She had been too ill to get up that morning and we had to shake her into consciousness. She looked round with dazed eyes as we told her to arise.'

Mary Lefley screamed and wailed all the way to the scaffold, crying, 'God knows I am innocent'. She yelled that if they hanged her they would be committing murder.

Berry said that nine years after her death, a farmer confessed to the crime on his deathbed. Berry must have lost the ability to enjoy a peaceful night's sleep after that; it had been a horrible experience, hanging a woman screaming out her innocence as the bell tolled for her death and crowd outside hushed for a few seconds.

The Man they could not Hang

Berry's most celebrated failure was in the case of John Lee at Exeter gaol. This happened in February 1885. Lee was just 19 and was convicted for the murder of his female employee; on the first attempt to hang him, the lever was pulled but there was no movement on the trapdoor. The young man had to be returned to the death cell until adjustments were made. Back he came again, and the same thing happened again. Lee was taken away again. One final attempt was made, and still the trap would not open. The whole affair was aborted until a decision was made higher up the chain of authority. He was, understandably, spared any other execution session and was reprieved. It was later discovered that a hinge had failed to work.

The chaplain expressed the situation succinctly: 'For the third time I had concluded the service; for the third time the prisoner had felt the agonies of death; for the third time the responsible officers had failed to put him to death.' Lee was released in December 1907 and married a nurse, but the relationship did not work out. We know that he died in America, forgotten. But since then historians have written extensively about the case. Poor Berry simply wrote, 'The noise of the bolts could plainly be heard but the doors did not fall.'

The Norwich Fiasco

Berry had a most horrendous experience in the attempted hanging of Robert Goodale at Norwich in 1885. The murderer was a very large man

The cells along the execution suite, convict prison.

– 15st in weight – and the drop calculation was wrong. Goodale was decapitated. The terrible business made Berry resign from his post. He wrote: 'The warder who had been assisting me had been standing too near the trap door, and the weight of the victim had pulled him over. He was clutching the sides of the opening, and it was only by the mercy of providence that he did not crash down to the foot of the well. It was the first accident of the kind that I had ever had, and I was unable to go to his assistance. Hand and brain refused to move. I stood there as if rooted to the spot…'

Berry carried out his last execution in Winchester in August 1891, hanging Edward Fawcett. But his own last years were a sad contrast. He was at one point suicidal (something common to many hangmen) and by an amazing intervention of fate he was saved. As he sat on the station platform waiting to take the Bradford to Leeds train, intending to hurl himself out of the carriage as it passed through a tunnel, he prayed and said to himself, 'Mother, I have not a single friend in the world…' Miraculously, a man who came on to the scene at that moment was an evangelist, and after they spoke they both wept and prayed together, a crowd gathering.

The hangman returned to his daily life, facing up to his lowly position. A large element of his depression was caused by the fact that people in the city knew his former profession and he was reviled and ignored by all. Berry himself became an evangelist. He spoke at various venues across the north, but he also took up farming in a small way.

He died on 21 October 1913, and in his obituary there was a reference to his pathetic years when he was desperate for cash as well as respect: 'A native of Bradford, he was widely known in the district, and the writer remembers one occasion when Berry offered to sell him a cigar case which had belonged to a person he had executed. It is well known that several years ago he was involved in litigation regarding the sale of a rope….'

Berry's life and work make a truly fascinating story, and that narrative helps us to understand what made men do that nasty, stressful and extremely maligned kind of work. The public hangman, through history, has always been a mythic figure in popular culture, almost as reviled and detested as 'Boney' Bonaparte or the demonic Mr Punch.

NINETEEN

William Scruton: the Bradford Historian

'There is a history in all men's lives'
Shakespeare

On 12 July 1878 The Bradford Historical and Antiquarian Society was formed. The founder members were J. Horsfall Turner, T.T. Empsall, William Cudworth and William Scruton. The last name resonates through the records of that particular variety of local and social history which looks into everyday things and everyday places in order to tease out significance. Scruton, for many Yorkshire writers and scholars, was the epitome of that kind of history that mixes antiquarian obscurity and detail with the central story of his age.

He lived a long and busy life, being born in Little Horton Green on 24 April 1840 and dying in Bradford in 1924. His life almost shadowed that of another great Victorian, Thomas Hardy, and each in his own way saw the depth of interest in the immediate past and the forces that shaped their contemporary worlds. He lies in Scholemoor Cemetery, but is not forgotten in Bradford. It would be very difficult not to come across his name if one went to the Bradford libraries in search of the city's past. The Yorkshire historians of his time worked in a network of writers, sharing interests, being involved in publications and disseminating knowledge with that spirit of enquiry and excitement which assumes that someone somewhere will find the footnotes of history useful to a project or as a satisfactory closure to an ongoing enquiry.

Little Horton Green in Victorian Times

As Jack Reynolds wrote in 1985 when one of Scruton's books was reprinted, 'To live in Little Horton Green…was in itself something of a stimulus to a lively mind and an historical imagination.' The place was a little patch of frozen time, an enclave which had in some respects avoided the modern urban development going on all around it in the city. Within the area were the Horton Old Hall and Horton Hall, and wrapped around the piece of more ancient Bradford was the new doctrine of self-help and improvement. There may have been plenty of old dwellings there, but young Scruton had a father who brought the past alive and kindled that historical imagination that was to forge a life-long interest and a passionate engagement with Bradford's history in Scruton's life.

His father had experienced the drama of life in the Leeds and Bradford conurbation in the Regency years, the period of radicalism and social unrest; the youthful writer would absorb all that and use the knowledge when required in his writing. Scruton exemplifies the autodidact, a common figure in that time: a self-taught man who read widely, thought, talked and cultivated what we would now call the study of the humanities. He learned much of that foundation of knowledge where the Brontë sisters also did – the Mechanics' Institute.

Scruton worked as a clerk and later as chief cashier, being employed at the company of Jeffreys solicitors. There he stayed all his long working life. We can find in Scruton that type of young man of the later Victorian decades who accepted the idea that cultural pursuits were desirable, but needed an arena, a fruitful ambience in which to be used and implemented to some purpose. He met Abraham Holroyd, a cultured man and a popular poet who kept a shop in Westgate, and Scruton wrote a long essay on his friend, in which he wrote: 'It has been my pleasure, and privilege too, to be intimately acquainted with Mr. Holroyd for more than a quarter of a century. In my own antiquarian pursuits I have often been indebted to him for guidance and help, which were ever given freely and unstintingly, for he was indeed generous to a fault. As the years rolled on, the acquaintanceship gave place to a close and enduring friendship…'

Frontispiece to Scruton. (*Pen and Pencil Pictures of Old Bradford*)

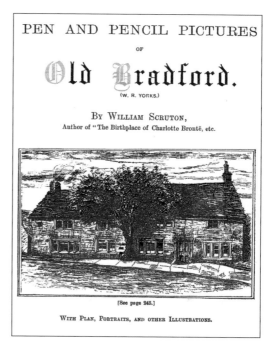

PEN AND PENCIL PICTURES

OF

Old Bradford.

(W. R. YORKS.)

BY WILLIAM SCRUTON,

Author of "The Birthplace of Charlotte Brontë, etc.

[See page 245.]

WITH PLAN, PORTRAITS, AND OTHER ILLUSTRATIONS.

Scruton was also a talented artist and that complementary skill helped in his work of preserving the sheer materiality of the past – public embellishments, street furniture and carvings, and so on.

The Publications

In his own lifetime, Scruton was best known for his book on Haworth, *The Birthplace of Charlotte Brontë*, which went through three editions in the first few years of publication. But in his *Pen and Pencil Pictures of Old Bradford* (1890) he produced what is arguably his special contribution to a very particular kind of history: that of the antiquarian. The dialect poet Edwin Waugh wrote to Scruton to tell him that 'I have been reading your book ever since I got it. It is an admirable production...' When we look at the book today, what strikes us sharply is that there is an attempt to understand and explain the most strange and inscrutable people and events, such as his comments on Mr Wroe the eccentric: 'Every afternoon the prophet Wroe held a kind of service to which he walked from Dudley Hill, in procession with 12 virgins dressed in white, and with long white tales.' When reading this, we can see how the footnotes of social history can become the data of folklore. Scruton understands that all the odd elements and influences at work on a defined community play a part in the uneasy mix that makes for continuance.

His Bradford history is very much about the people, organisations and historical forces which shaped the particular local landscapes, both physical and mental. That is, he saw that Non-conformity had created so much that went beyond the mere material evidence of places of worship. A good example is his use of sketches, because here we have not only the iconic places associated with Wesley or Scoresby, but such things as horse fairs, theatre memorabilia, toll bars and inns alongside the pictures of the worthies such as Salt, Nelson and Lister.

His ability to evoke and describe important public occasions is very skilful, as in this account of election time, always an excitable event in that period: 'On the day of nomination, the streets of Bradford were thronged with interested spectators, the neighbourhood of the White Lion, Kirkgate, being especially crowded with onlookers anxiously awaiting the appearance of the two Tory candidates, Messrs John Hardy and W. Busfield Jun., who were to proceed from here...the two gentlemen arrived and were greeted by loud and prolonged cheers. A Procession, four abreast was formed...'

Scruton was a representative figure of his time: an individual who took an interest in everything around him, and particularly in the vestiges of human community by means of seeing the importance of greater things through the material evidence of less important survivals of past ages.

Reputation and Achievement

Jack Reynolds wrote of William Scruton's *Pen and Pencil Pictures of Old Bradford*, 'It was one of three or four books which established the foundations of the history and historiography of Bradford. John James's work on the worsted industry and the parish of Bradford took the story just beyond the middle of the 19th century...Scruton provides a more general picture and brings the story very nearly up to the last decade of the century.'

He became very much what was thought of in his time as a 'bookman' as well, and it was a time in which those types – writers who could deal with book reviews, features for various publications and major works – could achieve a considerable reputation in spite of being 'all-rounders'. We can gauge something of the quality of his achievement by noticing that he has an entry in the prestigious national reference work, *The Literary Yearbook*. In the 1911 edition he is given as the author of five books and as a contributor to several newspapers and journals, and his contact address is 'The Whitelands, Baildon, Bradford'. He contributed to the *Leeds Mercury* as well as to the *Bradford Daily Argus* and *The Yorkshire Observer*.

William Scruton.
(from *Yorkshire Notes and Queries*, 1906)

Looking at his writings through modern eyes, from a time in which the writing of history has become a subject with various theoretical foundations, we can see that William Scruton made a massive contribution not only to the material sources of local history in Yorkshire, but also to such areas of interest as folklore, theatre history and popular narrative. As he said in the preface to the first edition of his Bradford history, 'As it was impossible to attempt anything like a complete history of Bradford within the limits of a work like the present, I have confined myself to subjects of the most general interest...' That selection was probably a struggle for him, and as it was such things as 'Early Bradford Wills' that were left out.

He perhaps never realised it at the time, but William Scruton was playing a major part in the documentation we have handed down to us about the formative people and movements in the West Riding, principally from the 18th century to his own age. Every historian has to create a process of selection, and that skill is maybe a more difficult task for the writer who is naturally drawn to the byways of history as Scruton was. But he managed to integrate that antiquarian narrative in a very entertaining way with the spine of genuine influences that made Victorian Bradford. Arguably, he saw the need to give the reader an account of major influences, but knew instinctively that small details interest us as well.

TWENTY

A Killing at the Orange Parade

'I've known Irish songs stir more than spirits – and evil ones
at times – sentiment turning to rage.'

J.C. Elias

Sometimes a song or a poem can indeed provoke a serious outrage, and one
instance of that happened in Victorian Bradford. It was common in that period
to 'blame Paddy' for most of the street violence around the northern cities. But
it has to be said that the media at the time took delight in playing up any brawls
involving Irish people. The hard-working navvies, like every other labourer of
the time, needed to unwind with a few drinks, and in the 19th century fighting
by beer-sodden men was not uncommon in Yorkshire. But this story has
nothing to do with that kind of scenario. It is a story of allegiances and honour.

In the midst of a series of terrible outrages against ordinary people in Ireland,
the year 1792 saw the foundation of the Orange order. The loyal Protestants of
the North of Ireland split the nationalist phalanx. That organisation would
prove to be the focus of a horrendous killing in Bradford in the early Victorian
period: the death and public fight had nothing to do with the Order as such, but
it was simply part of an ongoing antagonism in general, and Bradford happened
to be a place where many Irish had settled. This confrontation led to five people
being charged with manslaughter.

Images of the Irish
Behind this unpleasant and vicious attack was a contentious area of social
history: the nature of the Irish communities in the fast-growing northern

QUITE UNNECESSARY QUESTION
Newly-appointed Magistrate. " Any previous convictions **against the prisoner** ? "
A typical depiction of an Irish criminal of the time (note the facial features). *(Punch)*

towns. There were very large numbers of immigrants, of course, coming to Lancashire and Yorkshire to work in the textile industries. Social segregation naturally meant a process of ghetto creation, such as the area of Manchester known as 'Little Ireland' near the River Medlock. There were 34,000 Irish in the city in 1841. In fact Bradford had a much larger Irish population than Leeds, for instance, and that cultural presence was marked in the Victorian period.

The cultural and political dissensions and divisions, of course, came with the immigrants. The general population knew that the Irish worked hard and had built most of the roads and railways, but the image was unkind and harshly insulting, as in the appearance of Irish people in *Punch* magazine sketches and satires. Those images were often of men with simian features and brutalised natures. The events of 1844 would do little to counteract this negative image: an everyday march turned into something quite savage in the streets of Bradford.

The Brass Band in the Street
The trouble began with the members of the Calverley and Greengates Brass Band holding an Orange Day parade and moving in procession

through High Street, dressed in all the regalia of that order. As with all the garlanded parades of that era, happening every week, they carried flags and banners as they walked. Their repertoire for the most part was quite general and innocuous, but towards the end they began to play the melodies of *The Boyne Water* and *Croppies Lie Down*. Now the very word 'croppy' is almost always going to be potentially something to incite trouble. The song was always linked to the Orange yeomanry in the year of terrible repression in Ireland, 1798, after the Wolfe Tone rebellion. The song referred to the vogue of cropping the hair short, in a mimicking of the French republicans. The words of the song include a direct affront to these people:

'Oh croppies ye'd better be quiet and still
Ye shan't have your liberty, do what ye will,
As long as salt water is found in the deep,
Our foot on the neck of the croppy we'll keep.'

The Irish watching the march began to make a row and hoot at the marchers in derision. But the band went on and eventually arrived at their lodging rooms. The matter was far from finished, however. A band of thugs had waited for the right time to get some revenge for this provocation (as they saw it), and they had hung about until some band members dispersed and set off home. At about 8 o'clock that night the bandsmen were followed home, and in Eccleshall Road, near Airedale College, they were attacked. The drum was ruined and then the musicians were set about and severely beaten up. The assault happened quickly and took place ruthlessly, the villains running into the night, leaving a band member by the road side, bleeding and, in fact, mortally wounded. He was badly cut and his head was bleeding profusely.

The Attackers Apprehended

The poor man who died was one Benjamin Gott, and he died the next day, his skull fractured. It emerged later that the unfortunate man had been hit by a cobblestone. It had been a relentless and furious attack by a rabid crowd, on unarmed and defenceless people.

Five men were initially tried for the attack, followed later by four more men from Keighley. The first group were found guilty of manslaughter and transported. Prison sentences were given to the second group, and the whole affair was assessed and understood as what we might now call 'an isolated incident', but with hindsight and some more historical reference it is not difficult to see this as indicative of a deeper malaise, and one which had perhaps never really gone away. The general image of fear and mistrust in this period regarding Irish activities was never really erased, and such things as Arthur O'Connor's sensational act of confronting Queen Victoria with an unloaded pistol did not help to remove the bad press.

The Music Plays On

As for the general appeal of belonging to a brass band in Bradford, that did not diminish; as Gary Firth comments with regard to a photograph of a street band, 'They were big on volume and oompah jollity.' As old films and photographs confirm, the street life of Yorkshire towns at that time was as noisy, vital and appealing as anything in Shakespeare's London. As to the brass band itself, and its place in English life, only nine years later the Belle Vue open competitions in Manchester began: brass bands were to become more than a mere piece of street entertainment for northern people. But incidents such as this one in Bradford must have taught them to choose their repertoire more carefully. Of course, even the most seemingly innocuous tune might give offence to someone, but the croppy song being played that day was seen as an inadvertent act of provocation.

TWENTY-ONE

JBP: Bradford's Greatest Writer

'However poor you are in Bradford, you need never be walled in.'

J.B. Priestley

There are some regions of Britain that have been claimed for eternity as the province of a particular artist or writer. We always relate Thomas Hardy to Dorset, Catherine Cookson to Tyneside, Charles Dickens to London, and so on. Primarily, this has to do with the link in their work between their lives and their birthplace, but in many cases the writers in question do not actually live in their place of origin for long. Yet they are still organically a part of the history and heritage of the place in question. Such is the nature of John Boynton Priestley to his native Bradford.

As he himself said when he returned to the city to write his documentary travel book, *English Journey*, in 1933, he was not going to his Bradford. He wrote that 'his Bradford ended in 1914'. But the fact is that Priestley came to represent many of the essential qualities we commonly associate with Yorkshire writers, and, more than that, he became for a

J.B. Priestley. By Laura Carter.

time a national figure, a man who could, as he once boasted playfully, write an essay on anything from a lamb chop to a great artist.

Life and Work

Priestley was born at 34 Mannheim Road, near Toller Lane, on 13 September 1894. He had a long life and was one of the most productive writers of his generation. His father was a teacher and Priestley was imbued with a passion for learning and creativity, but early on he had to settle for clerking in the Swan Arcade, working for Helm and Company. When World War One came along, he signed up to serve in the infantry. Later in life he wrote about a reunion of some of his former fellow soldiers (in Bradford) and wrote tellingly of his army experience, particularly when he expressed his feelings about the men who could not come: 'They were with us, swinging along while the women and old men cheered, in that early battalion of Kitchener's New Army, were with us when kings, statesmen, generals, all reviewed us, when the crowds threw flowers, blessed us, cried over us...and then they stood in the mud and water, scrambled through the broken strands of barbed wire...and came back as official heroes...and now, in 1933, they could not even join us in a tavern because they had not decent coats to their backs...'

That passage says so much about Priestley the man and the writer: he was a ferocious fighter for causes, for moral issues and for justice. Many commentators have said that he was a writer and intellectual for the ordinary man, and there is much truth in that. Like George Orwell, he had that knack of writing narratives and essays which appealed to common sense and was strongly direct and often combative. Like Orwell, he was intensely aware of the effects of the English preoccupation with social class. At one time he wrote: 'I had been brought up in a West Riding industrial community, where to a youngster the social hierarchy was invisible... Wool men who gambled and won generally left Bradford before they acquired a title and began entertaining the County. If they had come back, a lot of men wearing cloth caps and mufflers would still have called them Sam and Joe.'

Assessments have stressed his massive output as a writer. Margaret Drabble, in her magnificent reference work, *The Oxford Companion to English Literature*, wrote, 'Priestley's output was so vast and varied that it is hard to single out his unique qualities. He consciously cultivated various poses – of grumbling patriot, cosmopolitan Yorkshireman, professional amateur, cultured Philistine, reactionary radical etc.' That sequence of phrases indicates uncertainty but in fact he loved to write with vigour, spontaneity and purpose. He was highly disciplined and ambitious, of course.

His fiction-writing life began with *The Good Companions* in 1929, and that was followed by *Angel Pavement* (1930), *Festival at Farbridge* (1951) and many others. His books of essays came into print thick and fast, notably his book of the texts of wartime broadcasts, *Postscripts*. But his plays are perhaps the works by which he is best known, as generations of schoolchildren have studied and written about *An Inspector Calls* (1947) and his plays concerning theories of time were expressed in *Dangerous Corner, I Have Been Here Before*, and *Time and the Conways*, all written in the 1930s.

Priestley also enjoyed creative non-fiction and was quite at home with producing surveys of social and cultural history, such as his successful work *The Edwardians* and his several autobiographical books in which he deals with his early years in Bradford. There are so many books of essays to his name that they are still easy to find in second-hand bookshops and, although many are ephemeral and tied very much to the literary concerns of a specific period, collections of these continue to be reprinted from time to time.

His entry into the profession of novelist was far from smooth; he began *The Good Companions* in 1928 and rushed into it without enough thought and planning, as he said that 'I decided that my story should be about a concert party and had to mug them up a bit'. He later referred to the book as 'the monster' he was planning. It took a long time to find a publisher for it, but he had confidence and self-belief in abundance.

The Writing Life

At one point, Priestley said something quite contradictory; that he lacked discipline: 'I have seemed to myself at all times to be lacking in determination and discipline'. But that was merely a sardonic glance at himself; he also said that ideas and themes were always there, and he had no sense of writer's block at all: 'Not all these ideas were good; many were indifferent, some terrible. But I have never been without them. They were just beginning to beckon then, about 1910; they are still beckoning now.'

As with so many writers, there was an influential English teacher at his school. This was Richard Pendlebury, a man Priestley described as 'Tall, intensely dark, as handsome and commanding as an ideal Spanish grandee.' The influence came from the fact that the future writer saw in him the love of good writing. So intense was Priestley's appreciation that he said of the teacher, 'Perhaps my feeling for literature could hardly be separated from my liking and admiration for Pendlebury himself.'

He was very skilled at describing and explaining the art and craft of writing; one of his most expressive images on the sheer hard graft of writing a book is his statement that 'Every morning you have to go in there and lift the elephant off the typewriter' and he adds to that the way in which the magic of creative writing and storytelling still happens: 'And because a lot of other people then must have felt in need of such a holiday, so long a daydream, the elephant suddenly turned into a balloon.'

Writing for him was clearly a business in which there were several matters weighing on his mind at the same time, and to understand his attitude to his work we have to imagine a cluttered desk and a full waste-paper basket. There is a picture of him looking though a book in his study, and the volumes there are teeming off the shelves, clearly in no particular order. But in the literary chaos he thrived.

The Freedom of Bradford and his Later Image

It is entirely in keeping with Priestley's later public image that there should have been a minor embarrassment over the question of his various honours. He did not want to have any honours, but did take the Order of Merit in 1977. But the question of his native city honouring him was something else, and it was down to the broadcaster Wilfred Pickles that this happened. Pickles said in an interview that 'If the reason is political…it is even more shameful…I love Bradford. I love its character and I love its forthrightness. That's not smooth talk. I mean it. And because I love it, I'll give you it straight. It is showing itself up because of Jack Priestley. He's an old man now – seventy-eight – surely they won't deny him this honour…'

The wished-for event happened in 1973, three years after the University of Bradford had given him an honorary doctorate. Perhaps some people who held that honour from him for so long had not read his work, and certainly not his work such as this passage from his account of 'T'Match': 'There are some parts of the West Riding that do suggest to you that industry is the supreme vandal, that the fair face of nature has been blackened; but none of these fine thoughts come to you in the neighbourhood of Bruddersford, where it is obvious that town and country are all of a piece and the tall black chimneys seem inevitable if fantastic outcroppings of rock on those steep hillsides...'

Jack Priestley's statue now stands by the National Museum of Film and Photography in the city of his birth. After the shame of taking so long to honour their famous writer, locals and enthusiasts from elsewhere surely welcome that prominence.

There was in him an indomitable spirit, and his words addressed to his fellow English people in the dark days of the 1930s surely seem indicative of the reasons why we still read and admire him; he said that it was for us to find our way, to look for the sun again. But in writing passionately, even in the case of his home city, he was never stupidly nostalgic, and wrote about Bradford in terms of the city he knew, when he felt the pull of the community to be strong and the sense of belonging always there.

TWENTY-TWO

William Edwards Escapes the Noose

'His case stands out in my memory, amongst those sad cases
I can never forget...'

Violet van der Elst

On 26 November 1936 William Edwards took the life of the woman he loved. Minutes before her death, she had been weeping for fear of losing him, so much did she love him too. Why Violet van der Elst found this story a sad case is that the young man had no idea what he had done. He was an epileptic.

The Killing

Edwards was 26 at the time, and a man who had been drifting from job to job since leaving school. He had worked at Tankards Mill in Laisterdyke, at Turners, the metal polishers and as a labourer for Sanda Metal Co. He had been working as a baker's assistant at Newboulds Ltd up to seven weeks before he took Myrtle Parker out for the night. He had known the girl for six months and they had been walking out regularly; he was always at her parents' house in Bierley.

Myrtle was just 20 and worked as a wool spinner; they had met at the Picturedrome in Wakefield Road. They discussed the possibility of getting married in May and she had agreed to marry him. At that time she was legally a minor (under 21), so Edwards had to obtain a form of consent from the Marriage Registry Office. He had talked about this with Myrtle's mother and she suggested that they wait a while. Matters seem to have been good between them, and there was no evidence of any acrimony.

On the fatal night the couple walked for about 40 minutes and then he left, but they met again at seven that night and, after spending some time at her home, they went out and stopped at Merrydale Road. It was there that, as they talked about their future, Myrtle began to weep and as he later said, 'begged me to stay with her'. This upset Edwards and tipped him over into an epileptic fit. He took out his penknife and opened it. The report from the trial has this summary of what happened next: 'His depression deepened and, as now appears from the reconstruction, he took up the knife and whirled his arm, not knowing where the blow fell. His memory failed him. He has no recollection of what else happened.'

Edwards did that with the knife and then wandered the streets until he arrived at a friend's house and there he slept: that was five in the morning. But in the morning he said to his friend, 'I have done my woman in'.

The Epilepsy Debate

Throughout the 19th century there was a continuing debate on what elements of mental illness constituted a defence of insanity and diminished responsibility. In a formative Lincolnshire case in the 1870s a psychologist called Maudsley entered the debate, and a man who had killed a village constable and had a death sentence was reprieved, as his epilepsy was shown to be the cause of his murderous actions.

In Edwards's case, he was sentenced to death, in spite of evidence from all kinds of sources. First, his friend, Mr Marshall, who had seen him arrive early that morning and had seen his pitiable condition; then two medical men insisted that Edwards's case fulfuilled

A letter on epilepsy in a criminal trial.
(*The Times*)

EPILEPTIC HOMICIDE.

TO THE EDITOR OF THE TIMES.

Sir,—Will you permit me to call attention in your columns to what you justly describe as a very painful case? I would do so in the hope that such further inquiries may be made by the proper authorities as your report seems to render necessary.

At the Lincolnshire Assizes just held, William Drant was tried for the murder of Thomas Bett Gell. On the evening of the murder he had been taken ill in a neighbour's cottage; he was cold, trembled very much, and was extremely pale in the face, crying out, "O, Lord, save me!" he begged some one to pray with him, and said to his mother, "Kiss me, Jane, I'm dying!" His mother kissed him and he kissed her. When he got home he lay on the sofa, feeling very sick, and his mother pulled his boots off for him. Suddenly he jumped up, exclaiming, "There's Jane," and, without any provocation whatever, seized his mother by the neck, throw her on the floor, dragged her about by the hair, and then, kneeling on her chest and brandishing over her a knife which he had pulled out, threatened to kill her. Four men armed with bars came to the rescue, and, after striking him on the head and on the arm, disarmed him, he resisting furiously. After the struggle he was quiet for a moment, then seized one of the pieces of wood which had been thoughtlessly thrown on the floor, sprang up, suddenly rushed out of the house after the men, and then, overtaking one of them, felled him with a terrific blow on the back of the head and beat in his skull with blows which sounded like "blows on an empty barrel with a lump of wood." When apprehended he was very violent, threatening to kill the first person who came near him. Afterwards, when charged with the murder, he exclaimed, "Oh, dear! Oh, dear! I didn't think I had killed him."

The mother's evidence, which is of extreme importance in regard to the interpretation of this unprovoked outburst of homicidal fury, is as follows:—

"When my son was quite a child he suffered from fits and has very much subsequently. He had two or three fits on the Tuesday night previous to this occurrence. On the following day (Wednesday) he had four or five fits. He the criteria of epilepsy: frequent headaches, moodiness and groundless loss of temper and a history of many such attacks. Of course, there was also no motive at all, as he had taken the life of the woman he loved and whom he wished to marry.

In court, the jury heard that four years earlier Edwards had wounded another young lady he was courting. He had stabbed her in the arm with his knife, and for that he was given six months hard labour. At that previous trial, epilepsy had been argued but had been ineffective. Again, when his life depended on the verdict, Edwards was let down and the judge placed the black cap on his head to pass sentence of death.

Other witnesses had spoken, such as a Mr Ogden, who said that Edwards had lived with him for a few years and that 'He used to sit in the house with his head in his hands. If asked to move, he would become bad-tempered, get up and bang things about…he would, for no reason at all, suddenly get up and bang things about…If asked what was the matter he would make no reply.'

The police surgeon, Dr Rimmer, said that his reading of the homicidal incident was that the man had suffered an epileptic fit. But one witness gave a clear account of a seizure: 'About a year ago I was out with Edwards in a public house. He was quite sober. Suddenly, and without reason, he threw a mug of beer at a man who had just walked past him. I hit Edwards on the side of the jaw. It was not a severe blow, but he turned pale and fell to the ground unconscious. He threw his legs and arms about and it was obvious he was in a fit. Two or three days later I spoke to him about it and he had no recollection of the incident.'

Hitting your friend on the jaw to help is a strange way to show concern, but at least it produced the kind of evidence that Edwards's counsel must have been looking for. However, it was all to no avail.

Even Myrtle's father, at the North Bierley Labour Club, saw Edwards in a fit and helped to carry him out. He and another man left him in the rain, thinking that would revive him. But the strongest statement came from Edwards's mother, Amy Edwards, who said that he had had two fits when he was just four years old and that he was three years old before he could talk. She said that as he grew older he would have frightening mood-swings and that he tended to fly into a rage if he was disturbed. He had left home in 1934 and lived with his sister, Mrs Ogden, in Lilac Grove Street.

The most considerable medical statement came from Dr Frederick Eurich of Edinburgh University and consulting physician at Bradford Royal Infirmary. He said at the trial: 'I have spent three and a half years in a large asylum controlling 2,000 patients, made a special study of mental diseases in England and in Germany…From the facts put before me, I have arrived at the following conclusion, namely that it is highly probable that Edwards suffers from occasional attacks of epilepsy…'

Eurich explained that people like Edwards suffer from loss of memory and waves of depression; he also added that in these states, the depression was likely to lead to periodic fits of violence. Apparently, Edwards lifted Myrtle over a wall after the attack but recalled nothing of that the next day. There had been complete normality earlier on the day of the homicide: Edwards had been at the home of Myrtle's sister, Gladys, and they had both walked to a draper's shop in Tong Street, where Edwards paid for some gloves he had ordered.

The Verdict

Edwards's last statement in court was that for as long as he could remember, he had never felt 'normal in health'. He also stressed that he drank very little alcohol, so that was never a factor in the violence. He was condemned to death, but that was overturned later by the Home Secretary. The campaigner for the abolition of capital punishment, Mrs van der Elst, wrote in her account of the case: 'I hope Edwards will be given plenty of work to do to keep his mind occupied, so that he can work out his own salvation.' She was one of the unsung heroes of the campaign against hanging, parking her large black car at the gates of prisons on execution day and making a nuisance of herself. Mrs van der Elst has given us the fullest account of the Edwards case, and her treatment of the facts was exemplary.

Not all killers in the throes of epilepsy were so fortunate. Also in Bradford, in 1934, Louis Hamilton killed his wife at Stott Hill and he was to claim an attack of petit mal, the less severe form of epilepsy. That did not save him from the gallows, and he had an appointment with executioner Thomas Pierrepoint in Armley.

TWENTY-THREE

Frederick Delius and his Apprentice

'There's sure no passion in the human soul, but finds its food in music...'

George Lillo

Frederick Delius is one of those composers who have staked a claim to be considered as one of the principal creators of English classical music – that variety of orchestral and choral music in particular that exploits the roots of music within the native traditions. In common with Vaughan Williams and Walton, he stands in that category of composers who left standards of music in that genre for the concert seasons and for Radio 3. His popularity received a boost when the director Ken Russell made a memorable film about his life and work, and in that film the amanuensis and acolyte, Eric Fenby, also received some acclaim and long-overdue praise.

The Delius of that film was cranky, moody and domineering, but he seems to represent for Russell that variety of artist whose personal qualities may be forgiven because the art itself is somehow heavenly and magical in its inspirational sources. Delius may have been individual genius, but he needed his Fenby. 'Fritz', as he came to be known, acquired a character in the media far beyond the reality of who he was and how he acted, but something about eccentricity becomes endearing to the British public.

Life and Work

Delius was born on 29 January 1862 in Great Horton. His German parents hailed from Westphalia and they were one of the many hundreds of families who came and made Bradford a 'Little Germany' in the 19th century. Music seeped into the family's cultural life and into their aspirations too. Delius's father, Julius, even arranged for Frederick to learn the violin, and the boy played before Brahms's friend Joachim.

He attended Bradford Grammar School and, like so many other artistic people from the city, he began the world of work in the wool trade, in his father's firm. But he switched careers completely and had himself sent to Florida: a genuine turning-point in his aesthetic development, as he learned something of the roots music of that area. He was there for over a year and he broadened his interests and his knowledge in both musical theory and in the practice of his art. He became after that a European, studying in Leipzig and in Paris. As one of the obituaries of Delius said, 'He took no part in the ordinary activities of English musical life.'

At Leipzig he met Edvard Greig, and it has been written that from him he absorbed a love of 'elusive polychromatic harmonies'. Delius married Jelka Rosen, an artist, and she had been seriously ill at the time Delius died in June 1934. His physical decline was serious: he started to lose his sight and also lost the use of his legs and, when it came to the point that he could work no longer, Eric Fenby stepped in and became the secretary who wrote down the music of the master from dictation.

Delius received many honours in his time, notably becoming a Companion of Honour in 1929; he was made a Freeman of Bradford and had doctorates from Leeds and Oxford. He died where he had been living with his wife for many years, in France at Grez-sur-Loing, and he is buried in Surrey.

As *The Times* obituary-writer said, it took a long time for him to find fame, but he had advocates: 'As a man, he remained entirely unknown save to a small circle of personal friends. Those friends have been declaring strenuously for the last 30 years that Delius was a great English composer...'

He is surely best known for his rhapsody on the old folk song, *Brigg Fair*, a song sung by Lincolnshire farmer Joseph Taylor whom Percy Grainger discovered. But also his *Walk to the Paradise Garden* has many enthusiasts.

Delius and Beecham

In the year 1907 Sir Thomas Beecham was the conductor of the New Symphony Orchestra and he was keen to bring contemporary music to the general populace in London; he introduced the works of Delius prominently in his programmes. He had not been the first supporter, as in 1899 a Dr Heym had given a London concert of Delius pieces. But Beecham really achieved the feat of putting Delius forward and his atmospheric music of place and the passionate attachment to locations of great beauty became Delius territory: such works as *Brigg Fair, Appalachia* and *Over the Hills* were slipped into the Beecham repertoire.

Following that, Sir Henry Wood also became an enthusiast; he gave the first performance of the *Piano Concerto in C Minor* at a 'Prom' concert in 1907. Then, at the Sheffield Festival shortly after that, the famous *Sea Drift* was introduced. Arguably the most successful event in terms of putting Delius and his work before the public was the composer's appearance to conduct his own *Dance Rhapsody* at the 1909 Hereford Festival.

In Covent Garden, it was again Beecham who led the advocacy, at this time with a more ambitious work, *A Village Romeo and Juliet*. In 1913 Beecham also conducted the stunningly original *Mass of Life*, a work with roots in the philosophy of Nietzsche. The general opinion of that work and its reception is, however, that it was truly understood when it was given much later in 1925 by the Royal Philharmonic Society, who also produced his Requiem around that time.

Beecham continued to promote Delius after World War One; some of the most memorable events in that regard were the series of concerts he gave at the Queen's Hall in 1929. Attempts to explain the specific qualities in the music of Delius have been made on many occasions, but perhaps most easily absorbed by laymen is the notion that 'The words are submerged in a sea of sound, and that not so much contrapuntal sound as deep and moving harmonic sound in which rhythmic shapes supply only a secondary interest.' In that, one can sense a number of mixed influences and traditions, from such works as Tallis's *Spem in Alium* to Vaughan Williams.

It has been pointed out that he used a wordless chorus as part of the orchestra too, as in *The Song of the High Hills*. But fundamentally, it is the richness of the sound in the orchestral works that makes his distinct signature. As was written in his obituary: 'It has been enjoyed as the music of a man who lived in a world of his own, yet who remained intensely sensitive to certain impressions from without and who gave forth again his impressions through his music.'

Bradford Celebrations – and Complaints

In 1939 there was an appeal for £5,000 to pay for the establishment of a Delius Music Room at the Bradford Grammar School, a Delius Festival was planned for the next year, and a new Delius Scholarship was being discussed. The appeal was led by various luminaries from the world of classical music, including Beecham himself, Malcolm Sargent and Eric Fenby. This sprang from an initiative just after the composer's death in which it was planned that Claremont, where he was born in Bradford, should be bought and a memorial placed there, but that was too expensive.

The new plan was to be part of a fresh development at the school, which was to have 23 acres of playing fields and, as was said at the time, that would provide a dignified setting for the memorial.

But in 1962, when it was Delius's centenary year, the aspirations were for a festival and in the Cartwright Memorial Hall there was a recital of his works. There was a grand occasion for that, with a champagne supper and a reception; a contemporary report commented: 'One could not help wondering how Delius himself would have regarded the mayor and civic dignitaries of Bradford celebrating his birthday in an atmosphere joyous with the sense of a local boy made good.'

Indeed, that was somewhat contentious. After all, he had not been near Bradford since he was a callow youth. As the celebrations went forward and the great Jacqueline du Pré played his cello concerto with Ernest Lush's piano accompaniment, there were some voices of dissent. A few months later, the music critic of *The Times* wrote a piece headed 'Illogicality of Bradford's Pride in Delius' and the writer pointed out that pride in Delius had its limits: 'But how proud can we deem the city which not only fails to mark Delius's birthplace with the appropriate plaque, but is reported to intend demolishing the Delius family residence in order to build a petrol filling station?'

On the plus side, however, the exhibition and celebrations in 1962 did give the public access to manuscripts and concerts; the highlight was the nature of Rudolf Kempe's tribute performances of the works. The opinion was that Kempe had done very well indeed: 'These three concerts have greatly enhanced Mr Kempe's prestige in Britain...the concerts have also confirmed Delius's claim to an honoured place amongst post-romantic composers.'

As to Bradford's general opinion and reception of Delius, it is not the only case of a 'local boy made good' who had nothing to do with the native city; if nothing else, the career and achievements of the great composer are a tribute to the German population of the city and everything they achieved in the arts through their caring and enthusiasm.

TWENTY-FOUR

The Pantomime Man: Francis Laidler

'Give me a laundry-list and I'll set it to music'
Gioacchino Rossini

There had been musical productions, revues, music hall and all kinds of cheap entertainment in Bradford for many decades before the main theatres opened later in the 19th century, but two landmark openings perhaps stand out in the years before pantomime appeared in its 20th-century form, and these theatre openings played a part in the necessary foundations for that seductive and happy form of theatre. The first was the Royal Alexandra Theatre, opened in 1864, and the second was the arrival of the Prince's Theatre in Horton Lane in 1876. These establishments meant that there would be serious and comic drama and that such people as Sir Henry Irving would come north, but they also meant that other, more democratic forms of theatre were possible. In other words, musicals always tend to come along wherever there is a stage, and the growth of the music hall entertainers in the Edwardian years also played a part in this.

Pantomime goes back a very long way in English popular cultural history; its origins may be found in the Elizabethan masque, but from Europe came the character of Harlequin and then later the great clown Joseph Grimaldi did new things with that stock figure. A landmark was the achievement of John Rich in 1717 when he appeared as Harlequin in a play called *Harlequin Executed*, which began the kind of entertainment we now think of as a pantomime. Most writers agree that the first

I'll follow him, all danger scorning.

A precursor of the pantomime – a Regency burlesque.

pantomime was staged in 1723 at Drury Lane, produced by a dancing master called Thurmond. By the 19th century the form was similar to the burlesque in some ways, as we can see in some of the dramatic comedies done by William Barnes Rhodes, such as his *Bombastes Furioso* of 1810, later illustrated by George Cruikshank.

Pantomime in Bradford

It was at the Prince's Theatre in 1902 that Francis Laidler began producing shows, and he was more enthusiastic for pantomime than anything else. By the Edwardian period, music hall was still around, but the attractive pull of what was usually called 'variety' was there as well, a form of entertainment for the whole family. Laidler was the man who was largely the driving force behind the building of the Alhambra, and his vision for the theatre he loved was to be a wonderful one.

Laidler was born at Thornaby-on-Tees in 1867 and he began his working life in a bank. In 1888 he moved to Bradford and worked as a secretary at Hammond's Brewery on Manchester Road. 1902 was the

A typical variety poster.

turning-point in his life, though, because it was in that year that he first invested in theatre: he had a lease on the Prince's Theatre and when his partner died it became his own business.

The Theatre Royal at the time was the foremost place in Bradford; one of his early productions was *Little Red Riding Hood* and it was a hit. Laidler, always the man with the commercial talent since the days of his partnership with Mr Piper, realised that he had a winning formula and that it would be well worthwhile producing a pantomime every season. In charge of Prince's, he tried a wide range of shows, covering variety and even melodrama. But he was always destined to be that figure we generally call an impresario or entrepreneur, and he stretched himself to take on the Leeds Theatre Royal as well. Pantomimes were now regular affairs in both Leeds and Bradford, under his guidance and control.

The Alhambra

Laidler's expansion in his chosen trade was always on a grand scale. As he was buying and planning his new theatre in Bradford on some land by the old Empire music hall, he was also developing the Hippodrome at Keighley.

In 1914 the Alhambra opened and Bradford had a building of great presence, beauty and style. It was a dreamy, huge concept, named after the famous Alhambra in Granada, the name meaning 'red castle'. Laidler thought about all the important aspects of such a place for a night's fun: it was heated by water and lit by electricity and gaslight; the stage was 35ft wide. The scale is easily grasped when we note that the seating capacity was 1,800 at first.

There were 11 dressing rooms for the performers. He was a hard-headed businessman who understood the need for comfort and good relationships with all professionals concerned in the industry. But he did have his limits in that respect, as may be noted by his refusal to allow his stars the perk of free tickets for friends. He had a notice on his doors backstage saying 'If your friends will not pay to see you, why should the public?'

The concept for the new theatre was rather more than pantomimes however. It was to be a classy, stylish place, with pantomimes left to the other theatres, and not until 1929 was there pantomime at the Alhambra.

Success on a Grand Scale

As time went on, Laidler needed support and partners who would be a part of his administration team, particularly after his marriage to Annie Uthank brought him a large family of four daughters and, of course, gradually more claims on his time. But the Alhambra was opened in grand style, and from that point he worked with Sir Walter De Freece, the best agent for popular theatre at the time. He was also the husband of the great artiste Vesta Tilley.

Five years after Annie's death in 1919, Laidler got married again, and the colourful and charismatic Gladys Cotterill, who was a young divorcée and just starting out in the theatre when they first met, but by the time of their marriage she had been transformed into the Welsh-sounding Gwladys Stanley – an affectation to take her image away from the very domestic and bland sound of 'Gladys'. There was Laidler, now in his mid-40s, married for a second time, but this time to someone not only in the trade and 'front of stage', but also a major name in provincial musical theatre; she had established herself at first as a principal boy in *The Queen of Hearts*, staged in Manchester in 1926.

One move that helped Laidler to increase his business and step up to the level of entrepreneur more generally was his union with the giant Moss Empire group, which had been a growing concern since the days of World War One, and it enveloped the role of booking agents for the new Alhambra. As for Gwladys, she appeared in *Aladdin* in Leeds and was engaged to a man who was one of the most successful and esteemed theatre and media characters in the country; he even lived in a hotel suite – at the Great Northern Hotel in Bradford. When she spoke about her life, Gwladys said that when she was appearing in *Aladdin* she had no idea that she was working in the theatre which she would one day own. It was to be a marvellous partnership in many ways. She was very à la mode and liked to fulfil the role of glamorous star, celebrated for wearing stylish modern clothes such as cloche hats and furs.

As for Laidler and his team, their pantomimes grew and grew, and his stars included Vesta Tilley, Norman Evans, Norah Blaney and Hetty King. Gwladys fitted well in that high company, jokingly saying at one point that she would never wear her white gloves in Bradford as the smog and foul air would ruin them.

Productions Large and Small

The years went by and the shows carried on, with some notable successes in the West End as well as in the north. After the first Alhambra pantomime of *Mother Goose* Laidler's horizons expanded, and in a few years he was producing the same show at Daly's Theatre. Then came a special pantomime at the Royal Opera House in 1939, and *Aladdin* at the Coliseum in 1940. He was producing theatre through the London Blitz of course, but 'the show must go on' and he was a determined man, driving things forward against all odds.

In Bradford, what became an institution was his troupe of 'Sunbeams' – this was a chorus of small girls recruited from the Bradford area, and the competition was fierce. One writer has noted that there were long queues of mothers and children all along Morley Street, hoping to pass the audition and become a 'Sunbeam'. The ones who were selected to work for Laidler would live a very comfortable life, and they also had a good education during the time they worked as dancers.

Some Stars

Undoubtedly, one of Laidler's major stars was the comic Frank Randle. Here was a tough performer, a man who had worked in the provinces in all kinds of halls and dives and done well, and then he had attracted criticism in the West End. He always had pulling power – not only for audiences but for women as well. Randle was born Arthur Hughes in 1901, a Lancastrian. He began with an acrobat troupe but soon worked on his own shows, which he called *Randle's Scandals*. Among other wacky escapades was his habit of throwing his false teeth into the audience. Laidler certainly had a live wire when he engaged the great Randle, a man who influenced so many later comics, including Ken Dodd and Morecambe and Wise. He will always be linked to his catchphrase, 'By I've supped some ale tonight!'

Sandy Powell also worked in Laidler shows, along with Albert Modley and others of that calibre: northern comics with a direct, genuine charm that seeped into their character and created a wonderful rapport with audiences of all categories. As always happens in showbiz careers, new talent had its chance locally and found a way through to major opportunities. It is to Laidler's credit that he gave attention to local talent

Another popular performer, Edith Ager.

Scene from *The Arcadians*.

and that he gave as much attention to the provinces as he did to the West End. Clearly, a succession of northern comics came through his productions and made names for themselves in other media such as the ever-popular light programmes on the new radio. Even the people who had been on the margins often did well, as was the case with

singer and writer Edith Ager, a star in her time and someone who was still in the theatre business, writing plays, working in radio and generally being a presence in the entertainment business. There were hundreds like her, in that age of new stars and the beginnings of the cult of celebrity we now see everywhere.

The End and his Achievement
Francis Laidler had seen his enterprises through the London bombings and through changing

The Coliseum today.

theatrical fashions, but his affection for the art of pantomime never flagged. He had gathered the nickname, or honorary title, of 'The King of Pantomime' when he died in January 1955. Sadly, he did not see the production of *Babes in the Wood* which was on at the Alhambra that winter season. Gwladys became the owner of his empire, and she was assisted by Roland Hill, one of the most trusted managers.

The end of the Alhambra as the home of pantomime came in 1964 when the Laidler company came to an end. Bradford City Council became the owners.

Laidler's career and his rise to fame and fortune illustrates the nature of the impresario in modern times: glamorous, stylish and successful, but again the story is a 'rags to riches' one, something the Bradford area seems to specialise in. The man who had once worked in a bank in Stokesley ended as a man who lived in a suite of rooms in a hotel. He had enjoyed a good, long life, and was 88 when he died. His empire in Bradford had lasted 56 years.

TWENTY-FIVE

Philip Snowden

'Philip Snowden, the Green Sea Incorruptible of the Labour Party…'
Roy Hattersley

Philip Snowden's political career spanned more than 40 years and in that time his fortunes and popularity swayed from hugely successful to almost rock-bottom. At the centre of his beliefs, after he developed into a socialist from beginnings in the Liberal movement, was the concept of ethical socialism. This was a belief that, in order to change the lives of everyone in all echelons of society for the better, moral views and actions were needed, but they could only happen if the economic basis of industrial society changed. That angle on political matters was to lead him into being a pacifist when such opinions were denigrated, and a feminist, yet one who upset some of the Suffragette leaders.

The foundations of his politics were in the life he knew in Keighley and in his home village of Ickornshaw near Cowling. But a glance at the main events and influences in his life shows some admirable achievements for a boy born into a Wesleyan family in a northern weaving village. He was MP for Blackburn in 1906 and for Colne Valley in 1922; he was Chancellor of the Exchequer in Ramsay MacDonald's 1923 Government, the first Labour one, and was still Chancellor in the later national Government of 1931.

Early Life and Politics
We know a great deal about Snowden's early life and about his growth into the acceptance of the political ideologies which shaped his consciousness, and we know these things from his autobiography of 1934. He was born on 18 July 1864 at Ickornshaw and his family were

Methodists with strong beliefs in education; Philip was at school in Cowling and also attended the Wesleyan Sunday School. He entered the world of work as a clerk in the insurance business. As a youth, he came to know the life and relationships around the world of work in a typical Yorkshire textiles community and he came to know nearby Keighley as well.

Many of his beliefs were grounded in the kind of morality which fused the Temperance Movement and the kind of radicalism he would have found in Chartism in its more intellectual expression. He actually met and listened to some of the famous Chartists and he wrote about some of them, but closer to home his own father was involved in that movement. Snowden wrote: 'I have heard my father relate how a number of handloom weavers contributed a halfpenny a week to buy a copy of the weekly *Leeds Mercury*, which was then sevenpence, and with these coppers he was sent to a village four miles away each week to get the paper...'

The Mercury, edited by Edward Baines, was a paper with considerable achievements in terms of radicalism and populism; Baines and his writers had, for instance, uncovered the work of government spies within the radical movements and Baines himself had been in Parliament. Even in Snowden's own village the men were observed by the local constable, and Snowden wrote that his father and friends had to be aware of being observed; when they met to talk they had a look-out and they closed the windows of their homes with shutters.

But it was education in the age of self-help that made Snowden equipped for politics and, along with his development as a speaker, he was soon acquiring the kind of knowledge a man needed then to talk and to be heard and respected. He explains his education after the 1870 Education Act in complimentary terms: 'The walls were covered with maps and pictures. Our curriculum was extended to include grammar, geography, history, elementary mathematics and the simple sciences...We were not troubled with the religious question...'

The Independent Labour Party

Bradford can boast that it was the scene of the foundation of the ILP in 1893. Snowden had been working for the excise and had been busy all across the land. He had also had an accident on his bicycle which left him handicapped. But in Keighley, the Keighley Labour Union was formed in 1892 and Snowden was active in the area, being elected to the town council. Working to make a socialist community around it, the Keighley group exemplified some of the key beliefs which surfaced in the ILP and Snowden was prominent in that, being an accomplished and powerful public speaker by that time.

Behind this growth there was a dissatisfaction with the Liberal regime and a Labour Representation League was formed. This was an intellectual platform, but in 20 years after that there was an emergence of a National Party for Labour. Snowden explained: 'By the end of 1892 it was felt that the various Labour Unions should be merged into a National Party. So steps were taken to call a Conference, which met at Bradford in January, 1893. To this conference delegates from the local unions, the Fabian Society…and the Social Democratic Federation were invited. There were 115 delegates present at this conference and among them was Mr. George Bernard Shaw, representing the Fabian Society…Mr Keir Hardy, fresh from his success at West Ham, was elected Chairman of the conference.'

From 1895 Snowden became notably active in promulgating the new Labour gospel, going on a long and arduous lecture tour, even visiting Scotland and Wales. When he came to do battle to enter Parliament, he did not look prepossessing but clearly had drive and energy. One account of him in 1907 describes him as '…small of stature and frail of frame, with a limp that compels him to lean heavily on a stick as he walks, he regards the world unblinkingly out of a pair of piercing eyes deep-sunken beneath and overhanging brow…' But he was a very talented public speaker and was counted to be on a par with Keir Hardie in that respect. He had a religious element as well, with talks entitled, 'The Christ that is to Be' and he gave a dimension of religious revivalism as well as new socialism. In 1898 he was editor of the *Keighley Labour Journal*, and so the foundations of his life's work were there: journalism and politics, and he was always going to earn from journalism, even if the politics failed.

Parliament

After failures early in the new century, he finally won the seat of Blackburn in 1906; the people must have recalled him from his energetic first attempt to secure their votes in 1900. Blackburn was Tory at the time and, as David James has written, Snowden 'mesmerised the electors of Blackburn. In ten days he swept Socialism from obscurity into a position which made it a serious contender for power'. Even with over 7,000 votes, he lost in 1900. But in 1906 he was Labour MP for the town. By that time he was also writing books on his politics: Christian Socialism was the key concept, and in books such as *The Socialist Budget* (1907) and *Socialism and the Drink Question* (1908) he showed that he had a sense of the practicality needed to link party doctrine to wider issues of how life was to be lived through moral worth.

Later Events: Ups and Downs of Power

In the period of World War One, Snowden was a pacifist and he lost much support and sympathy for that, of course. His personal life also played a part in his increasingly controversial position with regard to his political stance; his wife Ethel, whom he married in 1905, was an active campaigner for women's suffrage as well as for temperance reform. He began a worldwide lecture tour on the outbreak of war, and so avoided some of the worst repercussions of his perspective on pacifism and the war with Germany. When he was back in England, he did not hold back from expressing his views about militarism and warmongers. For him, the ILP was more important than the war machine; he made enemies of course, but lost a certain degree of trust even within the Labour movement.

When Ramsay MacDonald came to power as the first Labour Prime Minister in 1924, he made Snowden Chancellor. 'Our Philip' from Keighley was then a major figure in Government and finance was arguably his strength and speciality. However, he was in a difficult position as MacDonald's party needed the Liberals, and so his finance measures were somewhat stunted. He brought about some tax reductions but did nothing that might have been expected of a radical nature, rooted in Labour ideology.

In 1929 he was Chancellor again, and that was at the time of the Great Depression. He achieved some changes in the balance of tax payments across the board, helping the poorer classes. But the real problem came when he tried to reduce unemployment pay later on and, in the face of opposition, he resigned.

Perhaps Snowden's most telling statement about his beliefs and actions is found in this extract from his autobiography: 'I have always been an advocate of gradualism in social progress. 'Gradualism' does not mean that progress must necessarily be slow. The rate of advance must depend upon the intelligence of the democracy. But I do insist…that every step forward must carry with it the approval of public opinion, and that every stage must be consolidated before the next step is taken…'

After an operation in 1931 his health steadily declined and he was very much an invalid until his death on 15 May 1937. He died at Eden Lodge in Tilford, Surrey, far from that small village of weavers where his Christian and socialist ideas were nurtured, but his ashes were scattered on the moors at Ickornshaw. There was also a cairn built in Ickornshaw in 1938 in memory of him, and his huge collection of political literature is held at Keighley Public Library.

TWENTY-SIX

Maurice Wilson: Mountaineer

'High mountains are a feeling, but the hum of human cities a torture'

Lord Byron

When we read Maurice Wilson's eventful and enigmatic life, we have to reflect that Byron's words about desolate mountainous places would have found agreement in the adventurer's heart. Wilson was born on 21 April 1898 in Cecil Avenue, Little Horton. He went to school at Carlton Street High School and his eventful life began with his service in World War One. He was only 20 when he joined the West Yorkshire Regiment in France, and the fact that he won a Military Cross comes as no surprise when we reflect that he is remembered in history mainly for what used to be called deeds of valour. Through other eyes, and with another spin, his deeds were foolhardy. He won his MC when he confronted a German machine gun position and effectively flattened them and came back to his entrenchments with their weapon.

The Dangerous Solo Flight

After he left the army, Wilson worked for a while with a company called Mason and Dutton, but there was a restlessness in him and he was always destined to be arguably Yorkshire's most clear example of the old 'gentleman adventurer'. He was soon living in New Zealand, owning a clothing business there, and then he moved back home; at that time his interest in the new leisure aviation fad grew and he was busy obtaining a pilot's licence as well as running a business. But the call of adventure was there and when he had his licence he developed an interest in something far more ambitious than merely flying over the Lake District. Wilson planned to fly to India, and from there he would climb Mount Everest.

Amazingly, he achieved that feat, although at the time he was very much a novice flyer. This was in May and June in 1933, flying from Heston to India. He was at the time a member of the London Aero Club; he was 38 years old and determined to climb Everest alone. He wanted to climb the mountain and put a British flag on the summit. The opposition was very strong but Wilson was a formidable force in everything he did. When he arrived in India he began to prepare for the climb of over 29,000ft. He got himself to the base camp on the India-Nepal border but had no permission to fly further. His aim had been to land the plane at 10,000ft on the mountain, to give himself a head-start and save time.

Everest

Wilson began a training regime to prepare for the feat, training himself to live on cereal and dates. He also bought an oxygen cylinder and special light clothing – warm but very light of course. He also had a camera and a height-recorder to monitor progress. One of the main hurdles was the fact that he was virtually under arrest at Purnea, with his plane being held by the military until he promised not to do anything else and so sold the aircraft, a second-hand Gypsy Moth.

Naturally, he was determined to do the climb. He hired three porters despite the fact that the authorities forbade him to make the climb on foot. To avoid any trouble with the law, he came up with the deception of travelling on the route of a previous expedition led by

Maurice Wilson. By Laura Carter.

Feature on Wilson's expedition. *(The Times)*

Ruttledge and so, in disguise, he and his porters made it to the frontier; there he lost his porters and had to go on alone. *The Times* reported in July 1934: 'At the frontier...the porters were sent back to Darjeeling, Captain Wilson saying that he would go on alone. No news of him has been heard since.'

A few days later news came through to Britain that Wilson had been seen at 21,000ft, carrying a small tent, three loaves of bread, some porridge and a camera. The report on his last sighting was: 'He was last seen making off along a glacier. The porters were ordered to wait at Camp 3 for a fortnight. They waited a month, when they were almost foodless, as well as being ill-clothed for the height, and returned then to Kalimpong, arriving on July 7 and then to Darjeeling. Mr Wilson's advance was to be his final assault...'

Wilson was partly depending on finding equipment left by the Ruttledge party; from Camp 3 the track crosses a glacier and the temperature is minus 50 degrees. By 20 July hope was given up of any possibility of his survival.

The Route to the Mountain

Wilson's trek had begun with him in disguise as a Tibetan porter; he had disappeared by 25 March. He had managed to cross Sikkim by walking at night. In Tibet he could wear his own clothes again, and he was not molested or followed until reaching Rongbuk Monastery in April. He had achieved something quite stunning, even at that preparatory point: he had beaten the time of an earlier 1933 expedition by 10 days. That was achieved with just three porters and one pony. After staying a day at Rongbuk he went on to Ruttledge's Camp 2, then back to Rongbuk to gather energy and health before going on again. His last climb began on 17 May and, according to his porters, that climb would have ended around the level of 23,000ft.

Obviously, his porters knew all the routes well, and this story was told by them to the police back in Darjeeling.

Achievement and Reputation

Wilson's was the first solo attempt on the famous mountain. He had said before the journey, 'When I have accomplished my little work, I shall be somebody. People will listen to me.' But the records show that far more amazing than the Everest failure was the solo flight. For many years after, the remains of his camp were seen and photographed; a climber called Hemmleb has said that 'Occasionally you find pieces of cloth in the glacier that look like they could have come from the 1930s.' He has also found human remains; he has reported finding a piece of forearm and part of a femur.

The porters had seen that at the point near Camp 3 it was not possible to go any further, but Wilson had not been deterred and gone on. Eventually his body was found by Eric Shipton in 1935 and he was buried in a crevasse, hence the later findings of bones and clothes. Wilson had died of exposure and sheer exhaustion, most likely in his sleep. He still had food left near him.

Wilson had always believed that great expeditions often failed because they were too large-scale and were hampered by the weight of supplies. He had said that the man who would get up Everest would be an Indian yogi who 'had no possessions and was inured to simple living'.

As for Wilson and his attitudes and state of mind at the time, his diary says it all, because his last entry was 'Off again; gorgeous day.' The expedition led by Shipton gave the simplest memorial statement: 'We cannot fail to admire his courage.' Some people have called him 'The mad Yorkshireman' and in a strange way, that is a kind of compliment; there is a picture of him standing, arms akimbo, by his plane. He is tall, sturdy and resolute. If that was madness, then it has to be something to value. Maybe Bradford breeds men like that, and there should be an immense local pride in his version of 'madness'.

TWENTY-SEVEN

Writing the Moors and Fells: Riley and Sutcliffe

'Every chapter was written in my own home in the evening, as I sat in the easy chair by the fire, with my cloth-covered writing board on my knees, and my wife on the other side of the hearth.'

W. Riley

Halliwell Sutcliffe

Looking back at the Victorian and Edwardian years, one element in the literary world that stands out is the amazing status and popularity of those novelists who capitalised on the success of regional writing brought about by a range of great 'classic' writers like Sir Walter Scott and Thomas Hardy. One of these writers was Bradford-born Halliwell Sutcliffe, who wrote mainly romantic fiction inspired by the moors around him, his early reputation being partly that of a 'Brontë-inspired romantic'.

He was born in Thackley on 25 April 1870, and his father was a teacher and head of Bingley Grammar School between 1873 and 1901. Halliwell was at school there, and all around him were the moors, from Haworth, where he had lived as a very young child, to Harden. He may not have made it as an entry in most of the standard reference works on English literature, but in terms of Yorkshire writing he will always be a presence.

Literary career

When he died in Linton in Craven on 14 January 1932, *The Times* obituary summed him up in this way: 'He was very much an outdoor man, fond of rough shooting, a golfer, and a gardener, and he was in his element as president of the Yorkshire Federation of Rambling Clubs... He married in 1904 Miss Cotterill...of Twickenham; she survives him with two sons...'

This highlights his leisure, but we need to reflect on his personality to understand his writing; he was a good scholar and went to King's College, Cambridge, even though his subject was maths. But after some time in London, where he met his wife, he settled in Linton and wrote steadily, being very productive after his first novel, *The Eleventh Commandment* appeared in 1895. This was followed by perhaps his most influential works, *A Man of the Moors* and *Through Sorrow's Gates*. These two were serialised in 1903 and made his reputation and popularity secure.

It was his mix of historical and folkloric material that made his appeal in many ways: with the settings of Brontë country and the Vale of Craven being the rooted places of his imagination and the sources of his fictional muse. The Brontë country figures in many, perhaps most notably in *Ricroft of Withens*. As Derek Lister has written, his charm is in the fact that each place 'was brought alive by his acute sensitivity to local atmosphere, made real by his profound knowledge of local history'.

Adverts for Sutcliffe's book. (*The Times*)

William Riley

More recently, the success of 'W. Riley', as he was known as an author, has been phenomenal. His book *Windyridge Made His Name* in 1912 and, although his work is now out of print and forgotten by many, his presence in Bradford writing is hard to ignore and his autobiography, *Sunset Reflections* (1957) says a great deal about Bradford people and history in the early 20th century.

He was born at Bradford Moor in April 1866, the son of a bank manager, with whom William started work after school at Bradford Grammar School. But the Bradford entrepreneurial spirit was in William – he and his brother exploited the new popularity of lantern slide shows and went alone in their own concern. Riley was brought up a Methodist and became a writer late in life. He tells the story of the entry into the career of author and the birth of *Windyridge* in his autobiography. In the year before he started work on that book, he had the severe trauma of the deaths of his father, mother and sister, all within a few months. He had two sisters still alive and he and his wife went with the sisters on a holiday to Switzerland. When they came home, the author in William was about to emerge: 'It was when the short days of winter came along that the emptiness of the home became more keenly realised; one evening when the four of us were gathered around the fire, I said, "I tell you what I'll do, I'll write a story and read each chapter to you as I go along, week by week. It may help us to keep from brooding."'

That apparent ease and simplicity hides a plain but clever element of literary genius and acute perception, because he hit on the idea of the 'stranger in a strange place' theme. He said, 'I think I'll bring some London girl on a visit to Yorkshire and see how she gets on.'

It was one of those instinctively commercial ideas in writing that echoes a feeling of the time – the region and the metropolis. He knew both, of course, and so was following the old advice to writers that they should write about what they know. He set about the task, with no clear idea of structure or storyline beyond that first inkling. But he said that 'Like Topsy, it just growed.'

The story is set in Hawksworth on Baildon Moor, a place he knew and loved. Riley explains the appeal for fiction: 'No village in the neighbourhood attracted me as much as this; so, when I had made up my mind to bring my heroine from London and introduce her to the storm and calm of a moorland hamlet, it was natural that I should fix on this windswept village...'

With no real knowledge of the world of letters and publishing, Riley innocently jotted down the names of a few publishers and wrote the usual letter that all novice writers produce, and one letter went to Herbert Jenkins in London:

'Sir,

I beg to submit my M.S. Windyridge and shall be glad

To know if you consider it suitable for publication..

Yours sincerely,

W. Riley'

Mr Jenkins thought the book to be a work by a woman author and addressed his favourable reply to 'Dear Madam.' But in this way was born a massive best-seller of its time. We should not be surprised at this, as one review of the book had this to say: 'One thing is disconcerting is that the author should dare to be a man. With calm assurance he rummages about in woman's mind and pulls her heart strings...'

Bradford Town Hall, close to the heart of Riley.

Shipley Glen, inspiration to both authors.

A scene from one of Riley's novels.
(Frank Marston)

" Please, if you're Mrs. Tickle, t' P'liceman said would you read this."

So huge and influential was the book that, like a modern soap opera, it persuaded many readers that the setting was real and that the inhabitants of the village really were there in Hawksworth. When one fan arrived and enquired about a character, a local person replied, 'Aye, and I think nowt on it. It's nowt but a pack o' lies from beginning to end.'

Later Life

After that late arrival into the literary world, Riley was a professional writer for the rest of his life. He was still a Methodist preacher, as he had been for many years, but clearly his public wanted more and more novels like *Windyridge*, as Mr Jenkins did also. He moved to Silverdale near Morecambe, and of the tranquil life he now had he wrote: 'Silverdale is a tricky village that never loses its attractions for those who love beautiful surroundings. It got its name from a Scandinavian Freebooter...and when the sun shines on the white scars of Castlebarrow...and glistens on the branches of the birch trees you could well believe there is another explanation...'

But naturally with a Yorkshire writer, that place was never taken out of him and he continued to write about the Yorkshire dales and moors. He was undoubtedly one of the best writers ever to explain and describe late Victorian Bradford. He wrote: 'If its detractors regard the city today unfavourably, what would they have thought of the town as I knew it in my boyhood, when what was to become Forster Square was a congeries of dim and dirty alleys, all of them thoroughfares...'

Riley died at St Anne's, Morecambe, on 4 June 1961. His books are still easy to find in second-hand shops, because of their distinctively bold orange or strong green covers and the Herbert Jenkins logo of a centaur on the spine, as well as the black and white photographs inside with the text.

Both Sutcliffe and Riley, each in his own inimitable way, gave us the spirit of place and people of the moors around Bradford and Keighley in their time; the former in romantic vein and the latter more in the manner of *The Archers*. But beneath their fictions there is a rich, fascinating sense of regional belonging, rooted somewhere between history and folklore.

TWENTY-EIGHT

Digging up the Past

'The past is a foreign country – they do things differently there.'
L.P. Hartley

Sir Mortimer Wheeler was one of those enthusiasts we treasure in Britain – learned, populist, full of joy and celebration for his subject, and truly aiming to disseminate not merely the knowledge of his own science and art, but the pleasure in the lifestyle that work gives him. He became a media personality later in life but began as an academic in a newly burgeoning field. His handlebar moustache and wit won over readers and audiences in all kinds of contexts and situations, and he is in some ways of the same category of people as Magnus Pyke, Tony Robinson and David Starkey – those with such a deep love of what they want to tell us that we learn from them through the entertainment they give.

Life and Work

Mortimer Wheeler was born in Glasgow in 1890 but his family came to live in Saltaire in Moorhead Lane in 1894, and then moved to Shipley. He went to Bradford Grammar School and was the eldest of three children. As with the poet W.H. Auden, it was the scenery of the moors and dales which formed his inspiration to become involved in some way with the past within those rocks and soils. Baildon Moor was the centre of this source of knowledge and fascination. Wheeler was a talented artist when young as well, and along with the collection of Roman pieces from the past came his oil paintings.

The Wheeler family moved to London and Mortimer studied at the University of London where he gained a BA and an MA by 1912. He served in World War One as an officer in the Royal Field Artillery and he won the Military Cross. One of his first professional appointments in his area of archaeology was in Wales, and during his time there, among other projects, he did some work at Caerleon, near Newport, where the Roman remains are extensive, with an amphitheatre, barracks and baths having been excavated. Today those locations are tourist attractions. He was Director of Archaeology in Wales between 1919 and 1926. Following that he did the same kind of work in London, based at the Museum of London.

Wheeler's warm, outgoing personality was flowering all the time and Rik, or Rikky as he was known to friends, was becoming influential in all kinds of contexts. He had read Classics for his degree and so he had a fine foundation for studies in Roman civilisation; his specialisation for his MA had been a study of Roman pottery in the Rhineland.

He married Tessa Verney in 1914 and she too was an archaeologist; they became known as 'the Wheelers' by all their friends and professional contacts. With her he excavated such sites as Segontium in Wales, and the work at Caerleon was arguably the beginning of his popularity with the general media because *The Daily Mail* sponsored him. Biographers usually point out that such things made him professional critics as well as peers and friends, as the tendency to popularise academic disciplines always has its detractors – those who insist that the rigours of a subject cannot be maintained while having one eye on a good newspaper story. But the success in that respect was always going to win over young people to the study and practice of archaeology, and Wheeler was very much aware of that.

In London he had the opportunity to add a new dimension to the work in his area of expertise: training of fieldworkers and site practice training. He and Tessa began the establishment of an Institute of Archaeology with those aims in view.

In 1937 he became Director of Archaeology at the University of London, and from 1944 to 1948 he went out to India to direct an archaeological survey. Similarly, in neighbouring Pakistan he was involved in developing the Archaeological Department of Pakistan and the National Museum of Pakistan.

In the central period of his career, working in Britain, he was notable for his work at Maiden Castle in Dorset, pre-Roman investigations at St

Antiquarian Museum.

The museum at Caerleon where Wheeler worked.

Albans, and at a Roman villa in Lydney Park. In his home county of Yorkshire his most notable dig was at Stanwick in 1954.

Tessa died in 1936 and after that, when the work in India was done and he had married again, Wheeler came home and went into the last phase of his working life, being a part-time lecturer. This led naturally into his writing and broadcasting work. He became secretary of the British Academy and wrote not only his memoirs, but also seminal works popularising his subject, such as *Still Digging* (1955) and *Alms for Oblivion* (1966).

The Wheeler Room at the Royal Academy.

Legacy and Influence

Wheeler created a number of practical methods of fieldwork, most famously his grid-box system in which a dig site is split into grid areas. Each grid is excavated complete in itself, and so, as work progresses, there is a gradual revelation of the area, with a cross-section of the space made from the separate grids. This approach has been used in digs across the world ever since. It may seem entirely logical and simple through modern eyes, but someone had to think of it and that man was Wheeler. Another thing he did which is now common practice but was not so in the 1940s was to employ local women and university students on digs; this made excavations less costly.

In his media work though, audiences found that rare breed, the man who carries his learning lightly and tells a good story. He was a regular entertainer on the popular television programme *Animal, Vegetable or Mineral*, in which he appeared with Glyn Daniel, another great enthusiast for the subject. One of their highlights in a series called *Buried Treasure* was the time when the two archaeologists tucked into a meal that was a reconstruction of the last meal that the Tollund Man (a sacrificed body reserved in a Danish bog) had eaten.

Wheeler loved giving talks and lectures and even indulged in that business on ship cruises; he was almost what we now call 'a national treasure' when we speak of media personalities whom the British public find particularly endearing, and in 1952 he was knighted. He was also made a Companion of Honour in 1967 and became a Fellow of the Royal Society in 1968.

He died in 1976 on 22 July; he was 86 years old, dying at Leatherhead in Surrey. In some places it has been said that Sir Mortimer Wheeler invented modern archaeology. That may be going too far, but it would not be difficult to argue that he invented modern attitudes to the subject. If there is one event that typifies the influence and impact he had, it has to be the work at Maiden Castle, because there he used the weapons found in order to reconstruct the narrative of a particular confrontation in which the Romans were victorious over the force defending the fortification. It would not be too ambitious to say that he played a part in battlefield enactments. For Wheeler, however ancient the remains in question, the story behind them could be brought to life with a combination of hard work and the discovery of a good tale to tell.

TWENTY-NINE

Some Bradford VCs

'I have felt proud of that valour which, with their gallant allies, they have displayed on every field.'

Queen Victoria

In the midst of the worst phase of the Crimean War in 1854, Queen Victoria gave out her first crosses, and it was reported by writer Emily Moore in these words: 'The next day there was a distribution of medals to some of the gallant, but woefully maimed and sick soldiers, the mutilated heroes of the Eastern slaughter. The poor tottering fellows could scarcely stand while their grateful and gentle queen pinned their medals on their breasts. Some of the officers were wheeled past her in Bath chairs, for instance young Sir Thomas Troubridge, who, when both feet were blown off still fought for his country to the end, while his legs were held up to stop the haemorrhage...'

That passage says most of the things that lie behind the concept of the Victoria Cross: the extreme sacrifice and heroism and the sheer selflessness involved in the kind of deeds done by men in war.

The concept of the Victoria Cross, introduced in that conflict in the Crimea, has always been related to the notion of people doing extraordinary things in the face of danger. There is an element of mythic narrative about it, but the fact is that some of the recipients of the cross have indeed done utterly bizarre and incredible deeds, such as an officer called Learmouth who really did take bombs and throw them back at the enemy in the trench warfare of World War One. But in many cases, the awards have been given to those who saved lives while risking their own in the face of battle, and that certainly applies to some of the Bradford men who have been awarded the VC.

Corporal Samuel Meekosha

Meekosha was born in Leeds, but he joined the 1st/6th Battalion West Yorkshires and was soon at war in France. But here is an example of a man who never wanted the fame and the glory: his moment came when he was in a trench that was detached from the network and he and about 20 other men were in that position under relentless bombing. This was on 19 November 1915 and during of the worst confrontations in the Western front engagement; a bomb hit them and several men were buried.

At that point their position was vulnerable, as the enemy could see their movements, but Meekosha and others directly set about locating and saving the buried men; they had to act quickly and that alacrity saved the lives of four men, and it was done where enemy shells were landing very close to them.

His heroism was in the usual reports in the *London Gazette* and he was given the VC.

He went on to live through the war and he was married in 1917, to a girl in Bradford. After a spell in the regular army he went into business as a tobacconist in Bradford and then later tried the same thing in Birmingham, but he had fallen into obscurity as far as his military career was concerned; nobody except those close to him knew about his special honour. Here was a man who was dedicated to serving his country: he served again in the next World War, though only in the Ordnance Corps stationed at home in Lincolnshire. Such was his need to be unnoticed in respect of his award that he changed his name and became known as Mr Ingham.

Samuel Meekosha died on 8 December 1950 in Monmouthshire.

Thomas Maufe

Also a hero in World War One was Second Lieutenant Thomas Maufe from Ilkley. He was born there in 1898 and went to the Royal Military Academy in Woolwich in October 1915. When he was in action with a gun battery in France he won his VC. The *London Gazette* gave the report of the action: 'Under intense artillery fire this officer, on his own initiative, repaired unaided the telephone lines behind the forward and rear positions, thereby enabling his battery to immediately open fire on the enemy. He further saved what might have proved a most disastrous

2nd Lt Thomas Maufe, VC. By Laura Carter.

occurrence by extinguishing a fire in an advanced ammunition dump, caused by a heavy explosion, regardless of the risk he ran from the effects of gas shells which he knew were in the dump. By his great promptitude, resource, and entire disregard of his own personal safety, he set an exceptionally fine example to all ranks.'

Maufe was only 19 at the time. He later became a Major, but in one of the most staggering ironies of all modern military history, this hero was to die on Blubberhouse Moor, because he was in the Home Guard in World War Two when a trench mortar explosion killed him and one of his colleagues on 28 March 1942.

Matthew Hughes

Going back to the original awards, we have Private Matthew Hughes of the 7th Royal Fusiliers. He was one of the men who was presented with the award by Queen Victoria in Hyde Park in 1857. It was another occasion reported at the time: 'Sixty two men of valour received the Victoria Cross from Her Majesty in Hyde Park on the 26th June. Multitudes flocked to see the interesting distribution. The Victoria Cross is a very plain affair, made out of the cannon captured at Sebastopol; a little leaden coloured Maltese cross with a red ribbon for

Matthew Hughes, hero of the Crimea. By Laura Carter.

the army and a blue one for the navy. The decoration carries with it a pension of £10 per annum. The Queen, with that air of majesty and condescension so natural to her, pinned the cross on each brave breast...'

Hughes was one of the men lined up that day. He was born in Bradford in 1840 and joined the Royal Fusiliers in Leeds. He had a strange early phase to his army career, being demoted and promoted a few times before settling as private, and he took part in the struggle at Sevastopol. The quarries were deep indentations made by artillery fire, and in these most vulnerable areas of the battle Hughes won his VC. The report in the *London Gazette* points out that he went for more ammunition while under heavy fire, despite the fact that he had been shot in the leg by a shell. Not only that, but he saved two lives as well: '...he also went to the front and brought in Private John Hampton, who was lying severely wounded; and on the 18th June, 1855, he volunteered to bring in Lieutenant Hobson, 7th Royal Fusiliers, who was lying severely wounded, and in the act of doing so was severely wounded himself (by a musket ball in the foot).'

Hughes came home, received his medal from the queen and lived in Wapping Road, Bradford, where he kept a beer house. He died there on 9 January 1862 and is buried at Undercliffe Cemetery. It is heartening to report that his grave was that of a pauper and that now a fresh headstone had been placed there to do justice to his several acts of heroism.

Eric Anderson

In World War Two, Private Eric Anderson won his VC when working as a stretcher-bearer at the Battle of Wadi Akarit in Tunisia. In that conflict, on 6 April 1943, he went out into no-man's land three times to bring in wounded men. His battalion of the East Yorkshire Regiment had been making a dawn attack, with A Company in the vanguard. They came under mortar fire from well-hidden enemy lines. While some men had found safety behind a hill, others were left open to small-arms fire. Anderson tried to save as many as he could.

Unfortunately this award was posthumous, because this brave man was killed while doing this great heroic action. He was trying to save a life when he was shot. The report says, 'By his valour, complete disregard for his personal safety and courage under fire, he probably saved the lives of three of his comrades, and his example was an inspiration to all who witnessed his gallant act.'

His widow was given the cross in October 1943, and later his cross was given to his regiment. Eric was born in Fagley and had been to school at Thornbury Boys School. At home he had been in a choir and worked as a driver. His grave is in Tunisia, and he has the distinction of being the only stretcher-bearer to be given the VC in World War Two. On that fateful day he must have seen that he was a sitting target when he went out a fourth time. He was the only target the enemy had to shoot at.

THIRTY

Len Shackleton

'Len Shackleton hit six on his debut in a 13–0 win.'

Sir Bobby Robson

In England we love to make heroes of our footballers, partly because it is our national game and partly because playing the game at a very high level is a rare thing indeed. Recently, Bradford Park Avenue ex-player Johnny Downie said of Shackleton, 'He was a wonderful player...Shack, George Best and Tom Finney are the three best players I have known.' Bobby Robson rates him very highly, and at Roker Park he is something of a mythical figure, never to be forgotten.

Life and Achievements
In Bradford Shackleton will always be in the hall of fame of celebrated Bradfordians as well; he was born in the city on 22 May 1922, living at Horton Bank Top. He attended Carlton High School and was soon someone who was noticed for his exceptional skill on the football pitch, winning some caps for England Schools. He was just 16 when he went to London and played for Arsenal as an amateur.

His time at Arsenal provides us with one of those amazing stories we never expect where genius is concerned – he was rejected, and by a man who should have known better, the legendary George Allison, who thought Len was too short.

Back in Yorkshire, Len started to play for Bradford Park Avenue in 1939. In fairly recent years prior to that they had done quite well, reaching the fifth round of the FA Cup in four successive years, from 1928 to 1932. They had been in the Second and Third Divisions for some time, and so they were seen as a moderate team, but there he scored 166 goals in six years and he was obviously spotted by the talent scouts from bigger clubs. He won the first of his five caps when he played in an international against Scotland in 1945. It has to be recalled that, as well as playing for Park Avenue, he was working, doing some time in an aircraft factory and then as one of the Bevin Boys.

In 1946 he was playing for Newcastle United, and that is when Bobby Robson saw him; the match he saw was against Newport County in 1946 and Len scored six of the 13 goals in the 13–0 win. Robson has written: 'I saw that game – it seems incredible but I did, I was there with my father. I would have been thirteen years of age…' In other words, that means that if Len Shackleton played, you remembered it.

Len was destined to be a Sunderland player for the best phase of his professional life, being transferred there for what was then a huge fee of £20,500, after the earlier fee for Newcastle of £13,000. In modern terms, he was 'hot' in the football market. The Sunderland faithful loved him and he once famously said, 'I'm not biased when it comes to Newcastle – I don't care who beats them!'

There appears to be some disagreement as to his record at Sunderland. Some say he scored 101 goals in 348 games, others that he scored 98 goals in 320 games. But whatever the truth, he was as much a hero there as he was in Bradford. With Sunderland he played in two Cup semi-finals.

In those years he won his England caps, but he also figured in charity matches, such as the wartime one in which Derby County played Huddersfield. Guesting for Huddersfield that day was Stanley Matthews, while Raich Carter played for Derby. Len played with Raich that day, and Derby won 4–3.

While Len was playing for Bradford, there was a match in which the Avenue played Sunderland in a 2–2 draw. Raich Carter scored the two goals. Len was playing for Bradford that day and Carter's biographer notes that it was eventful for the Sunderland star. Talking about his goals, he writes: 'The first was described as "as good as anything seen for years." The second was more fortunate, being a sliced shot which went in off a post.' Ironically, that day Len must have looked at the great Carter without knowing that very soon he would be the next Roker hero.

The most prestigious Shackleton game may arguably be the international with Germany in 1954 when he scored one of the goals in a 3–1 win over Germany, who were at the time the world champions. He was clearly a man with an immense drive to win and to achieve; his friend Downie recalls, 'One game I especially remember was when we beat Manchester City 8–2 in the Cup and neither he nor I got on the score sheet. He was very upset.'

Len retired to Grange-over-Sands where he died in November 2000 at the age of 78.

The Legend

Like many great players, Len had nicknames. One was 'the Clown Prince' and he took that phrase as the title of his autobiography in 1956. To others he was 'Shack'. After an injury in 1956 he started a new career as a sports journalist, working for the *Daily Express*. As to his skill on the field, one of the best accounts is from a Sunderland fan: 'When Shack wanted to play there was no one who could stop him. His spellbinding tricks were magical.' He became known as 'The wizard of dribble'. Here was a man who had played with the likes of Jackie Milburn and Bobby Mitchell; the journalist Malcolm Hartley, in a recent celebration of Len when a special display on his life was installed at the Avenue, said, 'Apart from the adhesive ball control and breathtaking body-swerve, Shack could hit a ball. His slender legs could crack the ball like a Bofors gun.'

Commentators agree that his real talent was in close control and being given the ball at his feet so he could take defenders on. It was said that he was good to have on your side if you needed to keep the ball and players were watching the clock. Sunderland player Billy Elliott has said, 'If you played the ball in front of him he would just stand with his hands on his hips and he wouldn't go for it…'

Park Avenue Pays Tribute

In 2001 a special memorial to Len Shackleton was opened to the public in the clubhouse of the Horsfall Stadium. Len's son, Roger, came to the event, at which the Lord Mayor of Bradford, Mrs Phyllis Pettit, officially opened the exhibition. Mitchell Downie was there, and the public and fans could study old reports and photographs, enjoying some classic images of him in action on the field. Perhaps one of the most impressive comments about him was that he could bend balls from free-kicks like Beckham. One of his other teammates, Jimmy Stephen, gave a comment to those who considered Len as having a weakness when it came to heading the ball: 'They say he couldn't head a ball unless it was in the six-yard area. I remember one game for Park Avenue when I lofted the ball forward head high towards Len – and didn't I get a telling off! He wanted it to his feet all the time. He was a real friend.'

The press release included this tribute: 'His untimely death in November at the age of 78 brought glowing tributes from those who were privileged enough to witness the mesmeric skills which made him such as entertainer. It is hoped that this display will provide a fitting and lasting tribute to such a great player.'

Every club has its local heroes, and only the very special ones remain such heroes after being adopted by other clubs and fans; Len Shackleton will be in that limited list of names who meet that definition of the local hero that his home town wants to keep and claim. After all, Park Avenue had him for six years and there must have been thousands of other young men like Bobby Robson who saw Len Shackleton at the stunning outset of his career.

THIRTY-ONE

The Historian of Things Victorian

'Bradford…was the representative city of the textile belt which depended on it but struggled against its dominance.'

Asa Briggs

It would not be too pretentious to say that readers of popular history would find it hard to find information on the material life of Victorian Britain without the books of Asa Briggs. His book *Victorian Things* arguably set the scene for that variety of social history which drew attention to the everyday tools, pleasures and duties of daily life in the 19th century. On a larger scale, he could also explain and open up the abstractions of Victorian government, regional identity and urbanisation in works such as *Victorian Cities*.

Of all the founders of popular social history, Briggs has a strong claim to be the one who helped

Lord Briggs. By Laura Carter.

us to look at the clutter in the house as well as the ideas in Government reports.

He also has a very high status as an educationalist and has paid attention to the impact of the media and mass communications in Britain, taking the kind of broad view we had in the works of Raymond Williams and others. Overall, he has taught that curiosity about the past entails a willingness to look at society from the bottom up as well as from royalty down to the commons.

Life and Writing

Asa Briggs was born in Keighley in 1921, into a family with a long tradition of working in the engineering profession. But there was also farming in the family, based at Oxenhope. He was a bright, intellectual lad from early on and he won a scholarship to Keighley Grammar School, then from there he went to Cambridge. His studies at that university tell us a great deal about his future interests and specialisms, as he achieved a double first, combining History with Economics.

Briggs was one of the group who were involved in working at Bletchley Park on the Enigma code; he was serving at the time with the Royal Corps of Signals. Then, at the end of World War Two, he had a fellowship and then a readership at Oxford and worked with Churchill on his major volume on the *History of the English-Speaking Peoples.*

He was at Leeds as Professor of Modern History in 1955 and then at Sussex, and in the latter place he made his first significant step into the ranks of those educationalists who played a major role in developing the so-called 'new universities' of the 1960s – what many have called the red-brick higher education revolution. The nature of studying for a degree at a university changed radically at that time and Briggs was part of that change, in his position of vice-chancellor at Sussex.

Regarding the study of history, one clear pointer to the ways in which Briggs looked at the past, and then interpreted it, is in his preface to his book, *A Social History of England* (1983), written while he was at Worcester College, Oxford, as Provost. There he wrote: 'Social history has now become a favourite kind of history, and as its range and methods have expanded, it has attracted more and more serious study…There are dangers in the new approach just as there were weaknesses in the old approach...Yet the time is ripe for a synthesis, covering the centuries, difficult though the task may be.'

Clearly Asa Briggs relished that task. Producing a synthesis covering many centuries is indeed a very difficult task, but he saw it through. He was writing at a time when the media had tried a simplified version of the same idea: the BBC had produced the ground-breaking series, *The Long March of Everyman* just before his project.

More recently, Asa Briggs has been active in publishing, linked with the Open University and the Workers' Educational Association.

History in Broad Contexts

Interestingly, when Briggs wrote his influential work *Victorian Cities* in 1963, he omitted Bradford, devoting a chapter to Leeds. But in that chapter he says a great deal about his home city as he compares its growth and sense of identity with its near-neighbour. He shows in that work a fine ability to relate individuals to their periods, and he can move from street-level history to big ideas. In comparing the two great northern cities, he reminds us that Bradford had terrible problems in some very important matters, such as health: 'In both Bradford and Leeds there was a serious problem of public health. In addition to the ill-health caused by insanitary conditions and inadequate civil administration, there were recognised occupational diseases, to which a Leeds doctor, C.T. Thackrah, devoted a pioneer study in 1831. Thackrah contrasted the "wonders which science and art have effected" with the horrors which manufacturing industry had brought...'

This is entirely typical of the approach Briggs has to his subjects: he shows the interplay between the crests of the waves and the troughs in the cyclical flow of the historical process. After all, here was an historian who could take a panoramic view of English history and attempt to make sense of the various roots and causes of our national identity and self-regard. He had the skill to relate the contemporary to the past with alacrity and power, as in this comment from his huge social history: 'Thousands of acres of down and heath have already disappeared with the spread of battery farming, cereal growing controlled by chemical fertilizers and a grass monoculture supporting intensive stock-rearing.' That could be the language of an official report, so exact is the grasp of the problem – and its succinct expression tells us a great deal about Briggs the communicator.

Broadcasting

Another facet of Briggs's historical enquiry is his interest in the growth of mass communications. He has always supported the BBC and has said a great deal about the educative force of radio and television. His major work in this area was *The History of Broadcasting in the United Kingdom*, which appeared in the 1960s. He gave a clear and fascinating account in that work of the powerful influence of Reith and the foundation of the BBC in the age of documentary.

This was followed by two more works: *The Birth of Broadcasting* and *The Golden Age of Wireless*. The period covered in that sequence of volumes is from 1927 to the 1950s, and then he completed the story of his own time with a book called *Competition*. ITV appeared in 1955 and he realised that his account of the birth and growth of the BBC needed to be compared and contrasted with recent advances and with the social change effected by independent television; one could be partly right in saying that his book on independent television, *The Franchise Affair*, had an element of resentment and polemic in it. That is because it has been pointed out that he himself was a director of the network Southern Television – a company that lost its franchise in 1980.

Asa Briggs was made Baron Briggs of Lewes in 1976 and it would be easy but superficial to see him as a writer who looked back to early broadcasting with rose-tinted spectacles, fully in support of the ideologies of the early BBC phase, when television and radio were seen as potentially revolutionary tools in the march to educate the masses. But as has been pointed out, his massive and ambitious histories of broadcasting do contain that critical insight we associate with his Victorian studies.

Influence

There is no doubt that Asa Briggs has many solid achievements behind him. He has been involved with the arts in the widest sense for many years. As far back as the early 1980s he was active in the areas of local history and social history in positions far more high profile than simply writing books at home in his study. He was President of the Social

History Society from 1976 and of the Victorian Society from 1983. He is a Fellow of the Royal Academy and has had many honorary degrees conferred on him.

Currently, his massive stock of scholarly papers are mostly held at the Churchill Archives Centre and their catalogue of his publications lists no fewer than 27 major titles. He edited collections of essays in addition to his own major works, and his interests have ranged away from the central interests in Victorian studies and broadcasting into such concerns as the Channel Islands, Chartism and World War Two.

There will be much more written about this remarkable man, but what needs to be stressed is that, for most general readers rather than for professional historians, his real influence and lasting presence will be in that dissemination of the importance of history as a way of understanding not only the forces which have shaped the present but also in another way – that of seeing that the experience of the human race at all times provides fragments of a great narrative. In his case, the Victorian period provided so many interesting points of change and so many intriguing people that he looked at it as through a prism, and that is how he helped us to understand a period – from many viewpoints and with an open mind.

THIRTY-TWO

A Barrack Tavern Tale

'Hasten to be drunk, the business of the day...'

John Dryden

Mohammaed Akbar would come to rue the day he walked into the Barrack Tavern in Bradford in May 1965. The pub, on Killinghall Road, was close to the location of the city barracks and had been rebuilt in the 1920s in a mock-Tudor style. It is no longer standing, but when Akbar walked in for a drink he was going into what seemed, outwardly, like a typical corner pub in the city suburbs.

In truth, that is exactly what it was, but there were two sisters drinking in there on the night and one of them had a grudge against Mr Akbar. At first it was a case of an insult passed and some scowling, but it soon escalated. Elizabeth and Kathleen Duffy were in the mood for a fight, and the unfortunate publican was to see a most unseemly brawl break out in his lounge bar. The confrontation happened very quickly.

An attack

The landlord stated in court that he never saw Kathleen Duffy break a glass, but she allegedly did so, and within seconds, when he glanced at the man involved, there was blood all over his face and chest. Kathleen, it was argued, had cut him with malicious intent. Soon the two of them were on the floor, struggling, and Elizabeth, who had been in the toilet, came out to join in. She was said to have grabbed a bottle and hit Akbar on the head with it, with considerable force. A witness, Mr Hunt, said that he saw Akbar 'holding on to Kathleen Duffy' and that she repeatedly slashed him with a glass.

Two constables were soon on the scene and Elizabeth must have been very determined to do some harm, as she fought on, even with the police present. It all spun out of control and it never became entirely clear what the alleged 'grudge' actually was.

In court, Kathleen said that she had struck the man, but then that he had aimed a glass at her, cutting her hand. This drove her into a fury. Her main defence was that she was very drunk on that occasion and had no real awareness of how furiously she had attacked the man. Elizabeth's testimony was different from the landlord's. In her version, she had come from the toilet and seen Akbar tugging at her sister's hair, as Kathleen was crouching on her knees. She also claimed that he had kicked her hard on the leg as she struggled to pull him away from her sister.

The Barrack Tavern as it was. By Laura Carter.

Decisions

There is no doubt that Akbar came off worse: he had severe facial lacerations. He had been, as it is usually expressed in the context of a drunken fight, 'glassed'. Everything seemed clear, however, to the judge at the first hearing. He saw no case for self-defence in mitigation of Elizabeth Duffy's actions with the bottle. The judge's argument for this decision was that there was no precedent example of a sister using force to defend her sister in such circumstances. Through modern eyes, this seems a very strange and irrational point, and the judge appears to have made up his mind about the truth of the events at the Barrack that night.

At the initial trial the judge had said, 'There is no suggestion whatever that she personally was attacked, and it is my direction to you to approach this case on the footing that it is no defence for Lilian (Elizabeth) Duffy to say she was going to assist her sister.'

Of course, even with the judge keeping out of this decision-making process, the jury may have decided that the evidence pointed to a malicious and unprovoked attack on Akbar, but that counted for nothing at the appeal hearing. Elizabeth Duffy was discharged and the sentence quashed. In effect the fight in the Barrack tavern was like every other brawl on record: two people very much drunk and disorderly, being incited to violence by some normally small insult or perceived antagonism. It was only because the judge did not allow the course of events to flow as they would when perceptions were blurred, that an appeal followed.

But this tale has to be one of the strangest appeals ever heard on a Bradford case, one of those extraordinary affairs when a wayward and eccentric personality has an impact on a criminal trial and the repercussions are bizarre.

Bibliography

Books

Arthur, **Max** *Symbol of Courage* (Pan Books, 2005)

Briggs, **Asa** *A Social History of England* (Weidenfeld and Nicholson, 1983)

———— *Victorian Cities* (Penguin, 1963)

Burnley, **James** *The Romance of Modern Industry* (W. H. Allen, 1889)

———— *West Riding Sketches* (Hodder and Stoughton, 1875)

Cawley, **A.C.** (ed.) *A Yorkshire Tragedy* (Manchester University Press, 1983)

Campbell, **Marie** *Curious Tales of Old West Yorkshire* (Sigma, 1999)

Duckett, **Bob** *Aspects of Bradford* (Pen and Sword, 2000)

Evans, **Stewart P.** *Executioner: the chronicles of James Berry, Victorian Hangman* (Sutton, 2004)

Fielding, **Steve** *The Hangman's Record 1868–1899* (Chancery House Press, 1999)

Firth, **Gary** *A History of Bradford* (Phillimore, 1997)

Forshaw, **Charles F.** (ed.) *The Poets of Keighley, Bingley and Haworth* (Thornton and Pearson, 1891)

Garrick, **Frank** *Raich Carter, The Biography* (Sports Books, 2003)

Lax of Poplar *Lax, His Book* (Epworth Press, 1937)

Lister, **Derek A.J.** *Bradford's Own* (Sutton, 2004)

Moore, **E.J.** *Life and Reign of Victoria* (Nicholson, 1910)

Pontefract, **Ella and Marie Hartley** *Yorkshire Tour* (J.M. Dent, 1939)

Priestley, **J.B.** *English Journey* (Heinemann, 1994)

Rede, **Leman** *York Castle* (J. Sanders, 1829)

Riley, **W.** *Sunset Reflections* (Herbert Jenkins, 1957)

———— *Through a Yorkshire Window* (Herbert Jenkins, 1948)

Robson, **Bobby** *Farewell but Not Goodbye* (Hodder and Stoughton, 2005)

Royle, **Trevor** *Crimea* (Abacus, 2000)

Scruton, William *Pen and Pencil Sketches of Old Bradford* (Amethyst, 1985)

Stewart, Basil *The Literary Yearbook, 1911* (Routledge, 1911)

Taylor, R.Y. *Yorkshire Anecdotes* (Whittaker, 1883)

Wright, Elizabeth Mary *The Story of Joseph Wright, Man and Scholar* (Oxford University Press, 1934)

Newspapers and Periodicals

Bradford Telegraph and Argus
Illustrated London News
Punch
Yorkshire Notes and Queries
Yorkshire Post
The Times Digital Archive
True Crime Magazine

Primary Sources – manuscript

Burnley, James *Literary Recollections of Bradford 1870–1890* Ref: B792 BUR Bradford City Libraries

Websites

Bradford Historical and Antiquarian Society
Bradford Park Avenue FC
Criminal Appeal reports
Victorian Society